CROSSCURRENTS
PURSUING SOCIAL JUSTICE AND INTERRELIGIOUS WORK
SINCE 1950

CrossCurrents (ISSN 0011-1953; online ISSN 1939-3881) connects the wisdom of the heart with the life of the mind and the experiences of the body. The journal is operated through its parent organization, the Association for Public Religion and Intellectual Life (APRIL), an interreligious network of academics, activists, artists, and community leaders seeking to engage the many ways religion meets the public. Contributions to the journal exist at the nexus of religion, education, the arts, and social justice. The journal is published quarterly on behalf of the Association for Public Religion and Intellectual Life by the University of North Carolina Press.

The Association for Public Religion and Intellectual Life (formerly ARIL) is a global network of leaders, scholars, and social change agents who explore religious life, engage in intellectual inquiry, and lead ethical action in the world today. Their primary objective, especially through annual summer colloquia and *CrossCurrents*, is to bring together leading voices of our time to advocate for justice and to examine global spiritual and interreligious currents in both historical and contemporary perspectives.

A membership to APRIL includes access to *CrossCurrents* starting with Volume 58, 2008, though our partners at Project MUSE, monthly newsletters, early access to summer colloquium themes, a 40% on UNC Press books, and more. For more information, including membership and subscription rates, visit www.aprilonline.org.

This reissue of *CrossCurrents* was one of four issues published in 2010 as part of Volume 60. For a current masthead visit www.aprilonline.org.

© 2010 Association for Public Religion and Intellectual Life. All rights reserved.

ISBN 978-1-4696-6677-8 (Print)

CROSSCURRENTS

RELIGION AND THE UNITED NATIONS
Co-Editors: Azza Karam & Matthew Weiner

292
Religion and the United Nations—Introduction
Matthew Weiner

SECTION 1: SCHOLARLY INTERPRETATIONS

297
"Religion, World Order, and Peace" Ten Years Later
David Little

307
Religion, World Order, and Peace: An Indigenous African Perspective
Wande Abimbola

310
Religion, World Order, and Peace: A Hindu Approach
Varun Soni

314
Religion, World Order, and Peace: Buddhist Responses
Donald K. Swearer

319
Religion, World Order, and Peace: Jewishness and Global Justice
Jeff Israel

328
Religion, World Order, and Peace: Christianity, War, and Peacemaking
James Heft

332
Religion, World Order, and Peace: A Muslim Perspective
Abdulaziz Sachedina

SECTION 2: EXPERIENCES FROM FAITH-BASED ORGANIZATIONS

339
Sri Chinmoy's Work at the United Nations: Spirituality and the Power of Silence
Kusumita P. Pedersen

352
The Salvation Army and the United Nations — Being Good Neighbors
Carolyn J. R. Bailey

368
The Center for Interfaith Action and the MDGs: Leveraging Congregational Infrastructures for Maximum Impact on Disease and Poverty
Andreas Hipple and Jean Duff

SECTION 3: EXPERIENCES FROM THE UNITED NATIONS

383
The UN System and Religious Actors in the Context of Global Change
Josef Boehle

402
Bringing Communities Closer: The Role of the Alliance of Civilizations (AoC)
Thomas Uthup

419
The United Nations Development Programme (UNDP) Working with Faith Representatives to Address Climate Change: The Two Wings of Ethos and Ethics
Natabara Rollosson

432
The United Nations Population Fund's (UNFPA's) Legacy of Engaging Faith-Based Organizations as Cultural Agents of Change
Azza Karam

451
Child Rights Organizations and Religious Communities: Powerful Partnerships for Children
Stephen Hanmer

462
Concluding Thoughts on Religion and the United Nations: Redesigning the Culture of Development
Azza Karam

Notes on Contributors
475

CROSSCURRENTS

RELIGION AND THE UNITED NATIONS– INTRODUCTION

Matthew Weiner

This special issue of *CrossCurrents* is dedicated to exploring the relationship between religion and the United Nations, with an emphasis on providing positive examples of potential and actual interaction, and making an argument in favor of developing partnerships between the world's governing body and the world's religious communities. As importantly, if not more so, we also hope that the articles collected here will provide a platform for further discussion and action among UN staff, scholars of religion, and religious communities themselves. To our knowledge, there has been little documented in terms of this kind of three-way discussion, much to the disadvantage of all parties involved.

This short introduction will explain our basic orientation to the topic of religion at the UN, the thinking behind our designating these primary categories and the article selection within, as well as provide a compass for following the arrangement of the articles that follow. The conclusion will provide a more detailed historical framework and analysis.

When the co-editors first began thinking about this topic, there was relatively little in the way of official initiatives within the UN system to engage religion, and yet paradoxically religion was everywhere in its midst. Indeed, as the UN was conceived, scholars of religion and religious workers advocated for a spiritual and religious voice at the world governing body; there was little in the way of direct and official response. In this way, the official current involvement of many internal UN agencies demonstrates decisively the growing pragmatic awareness of and interest in the role religion can play in fulfilling its mission, however yet still under construction.

Although not organized discretely, the articles that follow fall into three broad categories: first is a set of articles authored by scholars of religion who argue for, and in some cases about, the role of religion at the UN. They do so mostly around issues of peace building, and we have chosen this focus to complement other pieces which come from UN program staff that are located in particular agencies that deal more discretely with social and humanitarian problems. Collectively, these articles provide both more abstract perspectives about the moral role of religion in peace building and the place of religion in civil society as it interfaces with the UN. They also provide a variety of particular perspectives that distinct religious traditions have to offer when it comes to peace building through the UN's auspices.

The second set of articles are examples of Religious Non-Governmental Organizations, more commonly referred to as faith-based organizations (FBOs), at work with the UN. The world governing body is, of course, a collection of nation states, steered by a collective process among them; it is also a set of connected agencies that address particular urgent human needs. As a kind of federated system, it inherently recognizes the need for diversity, debate, and input from sources other than nation states, including civil society. It does so primarily through NGOs, tens of thousands of which, with very different mission statements, register with the UN, with a goal of influence. What influence is understood, of course varies. While UN agencies seek to reach religious communities to fulfill their work, FBOs serve as a primary way (but not the only way) that religion officially works with, and impacts, the work of the UN. There are thousands of FBOs both locally situated and international, with diverse missions, all of which seek some way to interact with the UN to fulfill their own religious or spiritual mission.

The articles in the third section explain some of the ways in which UN agencies have begun to engage religion. These are personal reflections by program staff members at the UN who are, through their work as described here, helping to engineer a posture toward religious non-governmental entities in ways which help them to better fulfill their particular agency's objectives. They report on how their agency understands religion, the way engagement can help fulfill their mission, the success they have so far achieved, and an assessment of the potential, and potential pitfalls, of engaging this realm of civil society.

Through these articles, we provide a sense of religious moral frameworks for collaborative work, as well as scholarly perspectives on how particular faiths can interface with the UN. By virtue of the diversity of perspectives about religion itself, it also reflects, importantly for those in the UN who wish to partner with religion, on different ways religion is understood as an organizing force.

The three categories represent three different places where religion and the UN intersect; where the role of religion at the UN is being thought about and acted upon, by different kinds of actors and social structures. As will be immediately apparent, and as suits the nature of an interdisciplinary journal such as CrossCurrents, the authors of each category write from very different contexts and experience, not to mention mission or intent in their work. Thus, their tone also differs widely. UN program staff write their articles as administrators of the UN system and understand religion through the governing body–based lens. Scholars of religion write with the intention of elucidating the role religion could play at the United Nations and think through issues of religious moral teachings, ethnographic examples, and questions of secularity as they go. Writers from the FBO perspective are themselves in many cases religious people explaining the work their communities do from their own religious moral perspective; and to complicate matters, their understanding of the UN, while apparently straightforward from a secular perspective, may differ greatly from different religious perspectives. While this collection of articles works together as a way of pointing to a larger conversation about religion at the UN, these perspectives are different in terms of end goals, substance and, importantly, tone. We have intentionally let these distinct textures remain.

Within each of these three broad categories—religious scholarship, FBOs, and UN agencies—we provide a few examples that gesture to a far wider spectrum. We do not attempt to show a comprehensive picture, nor do we attempt to touch on all of the important variables in terms of religion, race, gender, and geography; it is simply too much to cover, even to catalogue effectively, in such a constrained space. Instead, the examples serve to orient us toward the range of ways in which religion's role at the UN is being considered. With this in mind, we have chosen particular examples per category as a way of demonstrating how very differently religion can be engaged by the UN (in terms of social structure, diversity, and moral teachings), and how very differently the UN can be understood and engaged from a religious perspective.

Each group represented here has its internal retractors, regarding the engagement of one another. Religious communities often argue for steering clear of politics and secular structures, as they define them, in an attempt avoid being controlled or forced to compromise on their core values. This is often seen in the context of being forced to work within the structures of secularism, modernity, and secularity. Often scholars who study public religion and secularity make the same argument. Another critique comes in the form of questioning how religion is understood by governing bodies, and the suspicion that the orientation itself favors particular social forms of religion, not to mention religious traditions. The question asked here is, who gets marginalized through the way religion is understood?[1] Finally, UN officials can question the value of engaging religion, when not seeing it as a social and moral force, or the danger of getting such relationships right. The editors have chosen not to dedicate a section to these arguments and instead allow them to run through the articles, with an important analysis by Karam in her conclusion.

The editors hope that these samples, and the larger categories that they do not so neatly fit within, provide material for further conversation about how the UN should think about religion, and how scholars of religion, and religious groups, can further think about and work with the UN. While we do not suggest a particular approach to this much larger project, we do wish to provide a framework for thinking about engagement, and do argue that this kind of engagement should be pursued.

We also argue that the three broad approaches outlined here should be in better conversation with one another. Indeed, we think that these particular examples serve as experiments, many of them successful, in the development of a more thoughtful approach. This issue of *Cross-Currents* wishes to call, through a small example, for taking stock of such examples.

Finally we argue, through the example of the pieces here, that a reciprocal educational process, where religious communities learn about and engage with, and therefore become a part of, civil society, and where civic and governing bodies likewise learn from religious communities, is a direction we can agree to move toward.

Note

1. One example of the negotiations between religion and the public sphere can be found in the debates between Jose Casanova and Talal Asad. Casanova's thesis is that religion and secular civil society shape one another when religion goes public through a reciprocal process. Asad claims that religion is necessarily structured by modern governmental structures when it engages in public discourse. See Jose Casanova, *Public Religion in the Modern World*. Chicago: University of Chicago, 1994; Talal Asad, *Formations of the Secular*. Stanford, CA: Stanford University Press, 2003. Casanova's work, and much of the discussion about religion in the public sphere, revolves around the work of Jurgen Habermas. See Jurgen Habermas, *The Structural Transformation of the Public Sphere: An Inquiry into a Category of Bourgeois Society*. Cambridge, MA: MIT Press, 1989. For theological discussions in favor of this approach, see David Tracy, "Theology, Critical Social Theory, and the Public Realm." In *Habermas, Modernity, and Public Theology*. New York Crossroad, 1992. For an important theological critique of why religion should not join civil society, or engage modern nation-states, see anything written by Stanley Hauerwas, for example, *A Better Hope: Resources for a Church Confronting Capitalism, Democracy, and Postmodernity*. Grand Rapids, MI: Brazos Press, 2000; *A Community of Character: Toward a Constructive Christian Social Ethic*. Notre Dame, IN: Notre Dame Press, 1981; "The End of Religious Pluralism: A Tribute to David Burrell." In *Democracy and the New Religious Pluralism*. Oxford: Oxford University Press, 2007; *In Good Company: The Church as Polis*. Notre Dame, IN: University of Notre Dame Press 1995; *The Peaceable Kingdom: A Primer in Christian Ethics*. Notre Dame, IN: University of Notre Dame Press, 1983. For another attempt to bridge the religious secular divide in the public sphere, see Jeffery Stout, *Democracy and Tradition*. Princeton, NJ: Princeton University Press, 2003.

CROSSCURRENTS

"RELIGION, WORLD ORDER, AND PEACE" TEN YEARS LATER

David Little

Problems and challenges as they looked a decade ago

Composed as the background paper for the Millennium World Peace Summit of Religious and Spiritual Leaders, held at the United Nations in 2000, "Religion, World Order, and Peace" had two basic purposes. It was intended to provide a general orientation to the subject of religion and peace by introducing key considerations and complications; it was also intended to identify some of the pressing concerns that ought to be addressed in any serious engagement with the topic.

The paper stressed that by initiating, as proposed, informal contacts between the UN and religious organizations around the world, religious and spiritual leaders need to appreciate both the promise and the frustration accompanying international efforts, like those of the UN, in the areas of social and economic development and the resolution of conflict. That would mean embracing at once an expansive spirit of cooperation and public responsibility, and a deepened awareness of the challenges posed by collaborative effort, both *among* different communities as well as *within* them. It would, in addition, mean taking a very hard look at the record of achievement of the different traditions represented and sharing best practices only after worst practices had honestly been acknowledged. The paper urged that religious actors be looked at as forces for both peace and violence and that an effort be made to account for and address the difference. It also called for attention to the constructive as well as the destructive effects of political, economic, and social conditions on religious thought and action.

Second, the paper listed seven "Topics of Special Concern" (TSCs), or areas of particular challenge, as urgently pertinent to the subject of religion and peace: 1. Treatment of Minorities; 2. Conflicting Interpretations of Religious Freedom; 3. Force and Non-violence; 4. Religion and Human Rights; 5. Religion and Public Life; 6. Coping with the Aftermath of Violence; and 7. The Meaning of Tolerance.

The objective of inviting retrospective reflections on the background document from representatives or scholars of six religious traditions is to reconsider how the proposed orientation and list of challenges look a decade later.

Where things stand today

As to the paper's general orientation, all six authors agree, or at least imply, that the desirable spirit of cooperation and public responsibility toward peacemaking and development can satisfactorily advance among religious and spiritual leaders only when combined with a clear-eyed examination of obstacles that exist either among different traditions or within the same one. They all find heartening examples of peace-oriented thinking and action within their respective communities, though most of the authors either state explicitly or hint that such efforts are by no means uniformly accepted within the communities they represent. In one way or another, all give fairly concrete guidance regarding what must be done to advance the peacemaking inclinations of their traditions over forces inside and out that oppose or retard those inclinations.

As to specific commentary on the TSCs, all seven topics are addressed, and several are helpfully reframed and expanded to include urgent issues not identified in the original paper. As would be expected, the responses overlap in respect to one or another of the topics and will be so reviewed. The comments of the authors will occasionally be used as a basis for further reflection on the topics under consideration and their implications for religion and peace.

Wande Abimbola takes up concerns jointly touched on in regard to TSCs 1. Treatment of Minorities, 2. Conflicting Interpretations of Religious Freedom, and 7. The Meaning of Tolerance. In addition, he combines his reflections with an urgent appeal for UN assistance.

He is particularly distressed by perceived abuses against indigenous minority religions in Africa, the Americas, and Australia caused by "shameful and violent" attempts at conversion by well-supported Christian and Muslim evangelists. This is the result of a failure to consider that "what some regard as a legitimate effort at peaceful persuasion, others take to be a coercive intrusion that unfairly threatens the right to practice religion free of outside harassment and disruption," in the language of "Religion, World Order, and Peace." Abimbola implies that most of the interaction between indigenous people and outsiders is an example not of peaceful persuasion, but of coercive manipulation of one form or another, and, as such, should be legally and otherwise constrained.

Given UN efforts during the 1990s in regard to expanding minority protections, Abimbola's call for UN assistance is appropriate. In 1993, the *Declaration on the Rights of Persons Belonging to National or Ethnic, Religious and Linguistic Minorities* was adopted, followed by the *Draft Declaration on the Rights of Indigenous Peoples* in 1994. These documents specifically call for the legal protection of rights in face of discrimination or coercive interference with the free exercise of minority religious rights, including those of indigenous peoples. Accordingly, they establish binding terms of reference for addressing these problems by religious and spiritual leaders and others. Abimbola mentions that some non-governmental initiatives have been undertaken by the World Council of Churches and the Vatican, but complains that they have not as yet borne much fruit.

If anything, the problem of protecting minority and indigenous religion has grown in importance over the last decade. As has been discussed in the growing literature on proselytism, the problem calls for some exquisite balancing of the rights of free expression and free speech and strict provisions against explicit as well as subtle forms of coercive interference. In addition to legal action, it also calls for sensitive inter-religious deliberation and agreement on mutually acceptable "rules of engagement" among different religions.

Both Abimbola and Varun Soni have something to say about TSC 7. The Meaning of Tolerance. As the original document pointed out, tolerance is not defined in the international human rights document, and therefore active inter-religious deliberation both as to what the idea means and how it is to be implemented in practice is strongly encouraged. One thing is clear: although the idea is not defined in the documents, it always appears in conjunction with the principle of non-discrimination, meaning that tolerance cannot be understood, at least from the perspective of the human rights documents, to condone unequal treatment toward those having a different religion or belief. Beyond that, there is much room for further collaborative exploration.

The implication of Abimbola's comments is that tolerance between indigenous and other religions like Christianity and Islam cannot satisfactorily be clarified without addressing the deep tensions over contradictory interpretations of religious freedom—the right actively to persuade versus the right to be protected from unwanted outside pressure. This problem remains very much on the agenda of religious and spiritual leaders concerned with peace.

The implications of Soni's comments for religious tolerance, based on the Hindu tradition, follow from his description of Gandhi's peacemaking model. According to Soni, Gandhi's life story of exposure to several traditions shaped his own religious outlook. That outlook features the notions of cooperation and reconciliation, mutual understanding and respect among religions, particularly because his concept of Hinduism consisted of a combination of notions drawn particularly from Jainism, Islam, and Christianity.

It is clear from the expanding literature on religion and peacemaking (for example, *Peacemakers in Action*, ed. by Little), that religiously motivated peace activists regularly coordinate insights from their own tradition with similar insights found in other traditions. They thereby exemplify, as did Gandhi, a high degree of tolerance, at least in one of its meanings: "catholicity of spirit."

But tolerance has other meanings that also need to be explored, the better to overcome or at least mitigate extreme, violent forms of intolerance. The primary meaning of tolerance is "to suffer, endure, or bear with" in face of strong differences. Despite the appeal of an open, welcoming attitude toward diversity within and among religions, points of sharp disagreement and division will inevitably occur. Techniques for coping with that reality are also needed, techniques that can help people live with, and even profit from, firm divisions of opinion. Although a pattern of "bearing with" is not always ideal, it is generally an improvement over fighting.

Soni draws a connection between Gandhi's contribution to the meaning of tolerance and the famous Gandhian commitment to non-violence, thereby touching on TSC 3. Force and Non-violence. He succinctly summarizes Gandhi's reinterpretation of one of the Hindu sacred scriptures, the *Bhagavad Gita*, in keeping with the principle of non-violence. Accordingly, Soni illustrates the operation of one version of a "hermeneutics of peace." That is an interpretative framework based on the assumption that the pursuit of peace by peaceful means is a sacred priority, and that it should serve as a basis for selecting, accentuating, and coordinating texts, doctrines, and practices from different religious traditions. It has, recently, become a subject of general interest in the study of religion and peace. It needs further examination, especially in a comparative mode.

James Heft's comments on the Christian tradition address critical questions posed by the original document regarding religious attitudes toward TSC 3. Force and Non-violence, as well as TSC 6. Coping with the Aftermath of Violence. Is force ever justified in trying to impose and maintain peace? How shall force be balanced with non-violent and other techniques for reducing conflict and for dealing with post-conflict situations?

Heft's overview of the variety of answers given by Christians, and particularly by Roman Catholics, over the centuries is a useful reminder of the complexity and variability of attitudes toward force and non-violence in religious traditions. The alterations in just war doctrine across the years illustrate the complex interaction of deep-seated non-violent sentiments with equally strong beliefs in the unavoidability of force under certain conditions. According to Heft, the non-violent dispositions of Christianity, virtually dominant during the life of the early church and subsequently represented by a minority of Catholics, are exerting a growing influence on church teaching. Increasing concern with means for resolving conflict as supplements to, if not substitutes for, coercive means shows that. Something else does too: the addition of a brand-new just war category, *jus post bellum* (post-war justice), understood as "the obligation to forgive and rebuild after a war." It goes without saying that attention to the place of forgiveness, accountability, reconciliation and "restorative justice" in post-conflict settings has only grown further since 2000. Consequently, the possibility for religious and spiritual leadership has also expanded since then.

The comments on the Jewish tradition by Jeff Israel and on Islam by Abdulaziz Sachedina both address TSCs 4. Religion and Human Rights, and 5. Religion and Public Life. Israel's argument about the contestability of the religious nature of Jewish identity raises an important issue unfortunately neglected by "Religion, World Order, and Peace." The document does speak of the importance of confronting differences within traditions as well as outside them, but it does not consider the general question of how disputes about national identity are to be settled, nor does it call attention to the problem of accommodating *non-religious* perspectives that might be present, especially in traditions not thought of in exclusively religious terms, like "Jewishness." Nor does the document mention the need everywhere to confront and rethink the appropriate limits of religious influence on public life, as well as the place for and extent of "conscientious exemptions" from public responsibilities.

These issues underlie discussions of religion and human rights and religion and public life. Human rights law is clear concerning equal protection for religious and non-religious belief, although there is some ambiguity over the status of state or established religions. Although they are not illegal as such, their usual prerogatives are called into question because, according to human rights jurisprudence, they may not discriminate against "adherents of other faiths or non-believers." What constitutes equal treatment and non-discrimination under state or established religions, and how far non-religious views should be accommodated, is of course subject to considerable controversy among different religious and other groups, as well as among states, and should be the topic of extensive deliberation among religious and non-religious groups. Such deliberation should also apply to the question of privileging religious over non-religious points of view in respect to things like the public advocacy of peace, a question of special concern to Israel.

A related question, raised, but not clearly answered by Israel, is the implication of his view of Jewishness to national identity. Sometimes, he appears to exclude not only religion as a mark of national identity but also Jewishness as well. "Jews, in my view, are left invisible to politics. And politics is rendered remote from Jewishness; being Jewish, in and of itself, proffers no justifications for any political claims." Does this mean that Israeli national identity is, on his view, not only religiously neutral but also ethnically neutral? If so, the implications for the state of Israel are obviously radical indeed.

But whatever Israel's particular view of the situation in the Middle East, he raises a subject of broad importance. The connection between religious, non-religious, and ethnic beliefs to national identity is an international problem that needs the urgent attention of religious and non-religious leaders and groups. It underlies many of the festering tensions found in cases of "ethnoreligious" and "ethnonational" conflict around the world, including the Israeli/Palestinian conflict.

Abdulaziz Sachedina's comments concerning the present state of the Muslim world similarly address problems of religion and human rights and religion and public life. In proposing a way toward "a better understanding between militant Muslim leadership and those Muslim governments whose claim to political legitimacy is challenged by their own citizens," Sachedina urges that the UN and other relevant international actors begin to appreciate afresh the implications of Muslim political culture for "universal notions of democracy, pluralism, and human rights." By that means, he believes, it is possible to rally "the support of Muslim peoples to various forms of democratic participation."

His argument is that deep within Islamic scripture and tradition, often in competition with countervailing themes, lie the foundations for a belief in "functional secularity" presupposing a public space "independent of religious presuppositions," and resting on common principles all citizens of a given state may be expected to share, regardless of their religious identity. These common principles include universal human rights and rule-of-law standards guaranteeing freedom of religion and conscience, women's rights, civil and political rights, constitutional government, and so on. As such, they constitute the criteria of political legitimacy for Muslim governments, as well as other governments. Sachedina contends that by carefully grounding these conclusions in scripture and tradition, his proposals have a chance of attracting strong Islamic support, even from the more conservative wings.

At the same time, Sachedina admits some tension between his proposal and "secularist, universalistic" assumptions that he believes underlie "contemporary liberal politics," assumptions that for him have very ominous implications. He thinks they exclude moral and metaphysical beliefs that bear on decisions in the public sphere, thereby precluding background commitments to the Qur'an and the Islamic tradition that even progressive Muslims would be bound adhere to. Moreover, they "absolutize" individuals and thus undermine public obligations necessary "for the smooth functioning of the political order."

In the interest of encouraging Muslim commitment to human rights and the rule of law, and yet doing that without denaturing Islam by preventing the influence of religious ideas on public life, Sachedina appears to proposes rethinking and modifying the "secularist, universalistic" presuppositions of human rights and rule of law so as to make room for a religious grounding of public life, albeit a grounding disposed to support a "functionally secular" public sphere.

Whatever one thinks of the specifics of this proposal, Sachedina is to be thanked for taking up a deep challenge underlying both TSCs 4. and 5. It is to achieve a reasonable balance between heartfelt religious conviction and a commitment to a public sphere governed by human rights and the rule of law. Suggestions like Sachedina's might become the basis for further explorations among Muslims, as well as among members of other traditions.

Finally, Donald K. Swearer, in his reflections on four "socially engaged" Asian Buddhists—Thich Nhat Hanh, Sulak Sivaraksa, A.T. Ariyaratne and Cheng Yen—takes up a subject not directly identified among the TSCs listed in "Religion, World Order, and Peace," though it was alluded to in passing. That is the concern of religious communities for things like environmental protection, poverty alleviation, economic development, and inclusive medical care, all, of course, seen as critical aspects of a broader focus on peacemaking and conflict resolution.

It is hard to overstate the importance of these matters in respect to the wider agenda of religion, world order, and peace introduced in the background document, and Swearer deserves credit for calling attention to the impressive efforts by Buddhist leaders to address them. As it happens, much important work in this area has taken place since 2000, work that demonstrates similar activity in other religious communities. For example, *Mind, Heart, and Soul in the Fight against Poverty* by Katherine Marshall and Lucy Keough was published in 2004, followed in 2007 by *Development and Faith: Where Heart, Mind and Soul Work Together* by Katherine Marshall. Like Swearer's examples, these recent books provide models for further work and reflection.

Concluding thoughts

As an attempt, at the turn of the millennium, to provide a brief overview of basic problems and challenges in the field of religion and peacemaking, as well as to identify several "topics of special concern," "Religion, World Order, and Peace" was a modest success. One bit of proof is that, with a few exceptions, the six retrospective responses pick up and elaborate on issues and questions identified explicitly or implicitly in the document. It did fail to consider issues related to the accommodation of non-religious belief or the bearing of religion on ethnic and national identity, or to focus adequately on the subjects of environment, poverty, medical care, and economic development, but, fortunately, several respondents properly rectified those deficiencies.

It might be observed that the responses gave little direct attention to religion and terrorism, a topic that took on dramatic significance shortly after 2000 when the Millennium Summit occurred. The subject is in the background of the discussions of war and peace in the Christian tradition, as well as of religion and public life in Islam and of religion, non-religion and identity as related to "Jewishness," but it is not taken up as such. Two things may be said about the lack of attention. Perhaps the subject is no longer of such overriding importance because, for many reasons, it is now looked at more in perspective than it was in 2001 and thereafter. The religious connections, while undoubtedly present, are more complicated than was at first thought, as, too, is the question of causes and remedies. At the same time, terrorism, whether religiously colored or not, will not soon disappear. Religious communities ought not turn their backs on the subject, particularly as regards the ways in which religion does serve as an inciter or promoter of indiscriminate violence. The issues involved are obviously an important aspect of TSC 3. Force and Non-violence. Religious communities (and others) ought to continue to reflect on the matter, if only because the challenge of combating terrorism constitutes an exquisite test for theories of force and non-violence.

It is interesting that aside from Abimbola's response, there was little discussion of the "world order" part of "Religion, World Order, and Peace." Abimbola gives extensive attention to the role of the UN in dealing with existing challenges to minority and indigenous religions, and he picks up on an idea much discussed at the time concerning the formation of a UN-oriented council of religious leaders. Other responses mention the UN only in passing. Because the Millennium Summit of Religious and Spiritual Leaders was convened on the premises of the UN, and plenary sessions and panels included UN officials, and provided a setting for discussions between them and religious leaders, it is perhaps worthwhile reaffirming this concern. It is hard to see how initiatives in the field of peace and development undertaken by religious and spiritual leaders can be fully effective or sustained without continuing interaction and cooperation with the work of international agencies such as the UN.

CROSSCURRENTS

RELIGION, WORLD ORDER, AND PEACE
An Indigenous African Perspective

Wande Abimbola

It is now ten years since the historic gathering of the leaders of the world's religions took place at the United Nations building in New York. A lot has happened in the world since then; the most despicable being the attack of the twin towers of New York on September 11, 2001. It is therefore a very good time, ten years after the gathering of the year 2000, to take stock of where we are and where we are going as far as religion is concerned in the world.

It is sad to note that it appears that the United Nations has not taken advantage of the gathering of religious leaders to put in place a consultative forum of religious leaders to assist with conflict and intolerance, which have certainly not diminished since the year 2000. Such a body of religious leaders drawn from across the world should urgently be put in place by the UN. This will help to address and probably reduce violent conflicts now going on in the world, most of which are borne out of religion or at least have religious undertones. There is also the need for the establishment of a United Nations Commission on Religion to examine the rights of the world's indigenous peoples. This will be a follow-up to the United Nations Declaration on Human Rights. This is an urgent issue since the shameful and violent conversion of minority peoples of the world has continued unabated. The indigenous peoples of the world remain powerless in the face of competing claims and onslaught of Christianity and Islam. Billions of dollars are being spent every year to eradicate the way of life and identities of indigenous peoples of Africa, Australia, and the Americas in the name of evangelism, which those two religions claim to be part of their holy scriptures. This age-old practice has led to what could be described as genocide or annihilation of the identities of indigenous peoples of the world.

The competition between Christianity and Islam for converts among the indigenous peoples of the world has resulted in violent conflicts in Africa and elsewhere between the adherents of these two religions. Three of such violent clashes occurred in Nigeria within the last six months, leading to the massacre of thousands of people. How can the United Nations pretend that such violent clashes are none of their business? To whom are the indigenous peoples of the world going to turn for protection or succor? The forcible conversion of indigenous peoples of the world has been going on for more than a thousand years. It is about time the United Nations Organizations and its numerous agencies begin to do something about it.

In fairness to Christian leaders around the world, there were two major conferences that they have convened to examine some of the issues mentioned earlier since the last couple of years. The World Council of Churches held its own conference in Geneva in 2004, and the Vatican convened its own conference at Lariano Vellitri in 2006. I was present at both conferences at which lots of recommendations were made, but nothing concrete has been performed. The Lariano Vellitri conference was convened by Pope Benedict XVI specifically to address the issue of conversion. The Pope wanted the religious leaders of the world to put in place a code of conduct for conversion of people from one religion to another. We are all patiently waiting to see what the Pope will do with the recommendations of the 37 religious leaders of the world at Lariano Vellitri.

Perhaps there is no better way to demonstrate the need for a world forum on religion at the UN than in the implementation of the claims of scientists on climate change. Most of the indigenous religions of the world are rooted on respect for the environment. My own religion, the Yoruba religion, for example, is based on what can be described as a worship of nature. We believe that when our divinities, known as Òrìsà, finished their work on earth, they then changed themselves to different forces of nature. Sàngó became thunder, lightning, and rain. Oya became the Niger River. Olókun changed herself to become oceans, while Osun and Yemoja became the Osun and Oogun rivers, respectively. Obatala is the elephant, while Ogun is iron. There are at least sixty-four trees that (or whom) the Yoruba people worship as divinities. Every hill, mountain, or river of Yoruba land is a divinity worshiped by some people. Numerous birds and animals are sacred to Yoruba people who worship or venerate them. The earth itself (herself) is a divinity. Human beings are themselves divine through their Ori (soul or unconscious mind) and Èmí (divine breath encased in our hearts), which are directly bestowed on humans from Òlódùmare, our High God.

There is quite a lot that the indigenous peoples can teach about the world in which we live. There is very little that we can achieve on the issue of halting environmental change or degradation unless and until we see the universe through the worldview of the indigenous peoples who regard themselves as the custodians of the earth and whose religions and way of life are intertwined with nature in all its ramifications.

How about human rights, on which the United Nations has put together a well-known and fascinating declaration? Not much can be achieved in this area unless the UN cooperates with religious leaders of the world. It is sad to note that in spite of all the efforts of the UN everywhere you look in the modern world what we see is not human rights but human wrong and suffering. Ifá, the sacred literature of Yoruba religion, defines human persons as ènìyàn (the chosen ones). All humans, according to Ifá, are the chosen ones—chosen to do good for the rest of creation. We should all live up to that challenge and do good rather than harm or violence to the rest of creation.

CROSSCURRENTS
RELIGION, WORLD ORDER, AND PEACE
A Hindu Approach

Varun Soni[1]

In the 1992 United Nations report entitled "An Agenda for Peace: Preventive Diplomacy, Peacemaking and Peace-keeping," the Secretary-General defines peacemaking as "action to bring hostile parties to agreement, essentially through such peaceful means as those foreseen in Chapter VI of the Charter of the United Nations." In Chapter VI, Article 33 of the United Nations Charter, peacemaking constitutes seeking a solution "by negotiation, enquiry, mediation, conciliation, arbitration, judicial settlement, resort to regional agencies or arrangements." For the United Nations, in both the letter and the spirit of its Charter, the focus of peacemaking is on conflict resolution, reconciliation, and engagement.

All of the major religious and spiritual traditions have long developed both internal and external mechanisms for conflict resolution. Accordingly, the world's religions offer processes and paradigms for peacemaking that go to the heart of the United Nations Charter, and that could be both instructive and instrumental in developing peacemaking approaches and mobilizing peacekeeping communities. The authors of "Religion, World Order, and Peace," prepared for the UN Millennium World Peace Summit of Religious and Spiritual Leaders, rightly recognized the transformative peacemaking potential for the world's religions, which are replete with proven models of peacemaking and peacekeeping. In our post-9/11 world, articulating these peacekeeping models and mechanisms has taken on an even greater urgency.

[1]Varun Soni is the dean of religious life at the University of Southern California.

To connect the UN's goals of peacekeeping with uniquely Hindu models, I will examine the *satyagraha* philosophy of Mohandas "Mahatma" Gandhi, who is the most famous peacemaker of the 20th century. By examining Gandhi's life's narrative through the lenses of globalism and pluralism, and by focusing on his creative interpretation of Indian philosophical doctrines and texts, an innovative peacemaking framework emerges. This framework provides a powerful model for UN peacemaking, one that draws directly from Gandhi's conception of Hinduism and its pluralistic possibilities.

Although Gandhi is popularly remembered as an ascetic who was deeply connected to India's villages ("a half-naked *fakir*" as Winston Churchill famously called him), his background was actually cosmopolitan and global. Born into privilege, Gandhi studied to be a barrister in London, where he first became interested in Hindu and Christian scriptures. After experiencing a racially charged incident on a train to Pretoria, Gandhi spent more than twenty years pioneering his *satyagraha* strategy in South Africa. When he returned to India, it was as an English speaking, British-educated lawyer, who had lived and worked on three different continents.

Such a background was critical in informing Gandhi's sensibilities as a Hindu. Indeed, more than any other public Hindu, Gandhi's Hinduism most resonated with the popular Hindu ethos of "many paths, one truth," an approach that reflected his own life story. Gandhi's construction of Hinduism as a unified tradition characterized by its multiplicity of approaches is a religious conception that is pluralistic at its core. In acknowledging that individuals may take different routes to reach the same destination, Gandhi's Hinduism builds into its framework mechanisms for cooperation and reconciliation, for mutual understanding and respect. Furthermore, given the fact that Gandhi had an elite education and a multi-religious upbringing, his conception of Hinduism was deeply shaped by other religions as well, most notably by the Jain doctrine of *ahimsa*, the Muslim tradition of *zakat*, and the Christian ethic of the beatitudes.

Gandhi's pluralistic and encompassing approach to Hinduism is evident in his reading of the *Bhagavad Gita*, a pan-Hindu theological text that he wrote about more than any other single subject in his lifetime. In the *Bhagavad Gita*, Krishna counsels Arjuna on the battlefield and tells

Arjuna that he must fulfill his duty as a warrior and fight, even if that means killing his own cousins. To address the philosophical dilemma of transforming the *Bhagavad Gita* into a peacemaking text for the Indian nationalist movement, Gandhi opted for an allegorical reading rather than a literal one. According to Gandhi, the battlefield represents the struggle of good against evil. This can be construed in an introspective manner for the individual but can also exist as a social paradigm for political change. Because the battlefield is only a metaphor, there need not be violent connotations in the *Bhagavad Gita*. In this manner, Gandhi's interpretation allowed him to creatively downplay the prominent role of violence that is unavoidable in a literal reading, thereby empowering him to promote his own antithetical agenda of non-violence.

There are many who dismiss the efficacy of Gandhi's *satyagraha* movement by arguing that it was actually Adolf Hitler who was responsible for ending British rule in India. Furthermore, there were many Indian advocates for violent insurrection that Gandhi had to contend with in his life, most notably Subhas Chandra Bose. For Gandhi, though, non-violence was the only choice because he believed that the process was as important as the result. According to Gandhi, violent action, regardless of the short-term outcome, is destructive and becomes the very cycle of oppression and injustice it seeks to eliminate. By focusing on the Hindu doctrine of *karma*, of action and causality, Gandhi argued that sustainable peace could only emerge through genuine peacemaking, for any violent action would ultimately result in a violent outcome.

As one of the most influential Hindus and peacemakers, Gandhi's approach to peacemaking is instructive for the UN in a number of ways. He demonstrated the strategic wisdom of creating pluralistic structures that build peacemaking into their frameworks. He showed how doctrines and texts traditionally thought of as antithetical to peacemaking could be creatively reinterpreted and reconceptualized for the purposes of peace. He proved that communities with contentious histories could come together over their common goals of peacemaking. And he utilized Indian philosophical ideas of *ahimsa* and *karma* to promote both the process of peacemaking and the goal of a sustainable peace.

In 2007, the UN General Assembly adopted a resolution recognizing Gandhi's birthday (October 2) as the "International Day of Non-

Violence," and this day could provide a platform for the UN to publicly and proactively embrace Gandhian peacemaking. The UN could incorporate Gandhi's Hindu approach to peacemaking by recognizing the symbolic and strategic advantages of building pluralism into its structure, especially when engaging in reconciliation, mediation, and dispute resolution. The UN could also support Gandhian inspired movements around the world by collaborating with prominent peace leaders such as Dr A.T. Ariyaratne, Aung San Suu Kyi, Desmond Tutu, and His Holiness, the Dalai Lama. Indeed, all of these aforementioned Gandhian paradigms, strategies, and approaches could be incorporated into a comprehensive approach for the UN toward peacemaking—one that emphasizes and embodies uniquely Hindu conceptions of causality and creativity.

CROSSCURRENTS
RELIGION, WORLD ORDER, AND PEACE
Buddhist Responses

Donald K. Swearer*

The following essay presents four outstanding examples of Buddhist leaders who have dedicated their lives to addressing the issues highlighted in "Religion, World Order, and Peace," the document prepared for the U.N. Millennium World Peace Summit of Religious and Spiritual Leaders. The authors of the document rightly point out that from a historical perspective the world's religions have served to constitute a sense of social solidarity but they also have contributed to enmity and violent conflict. Doctrinally, the world religions uphold ideals of peace and non-violence, but historically they have been instrumental causes of intolerance and discrimination. In the face of the complicated connection between religion and conflict, the authors call on religious and spiritual leaders to commit to mitigating violence and transforming it into constructive behavior in ways that involve rethinking the formation of the religious life, reexamining sacred symbols, and reallocating resources. While not ignoring contemporary instances of Buddhist intolerance and even violence, are there exemplary Buddhists who are responding in positive and creative ways to the challenge posed by the U.N. document? To answer this question, I shall look at four different examples: Thich Nhat Hanh, the Vietnamese monk credited with coining the phrase, "socially engaged Buddhism;" Sulak Sivaraksa, the Thai social activist and co-founder of the International Network of Engaged Buddhists; A.T. Ariyaratne, the founder of the Sarvodaya Shramadana

*Distinguished Visiting Professor of Buddhist Studies and Director, Center for the Study of World Religions, Harvard Divinity School.

movement, the largest Buddhist NGO in Sri Lanka; and Dharma Master Cheng Yen, the Taiwanese nun who established the Buddhist Compassion Relief Tzu Chi Foundation, the largest charity organization in Taiwan with centers in thirty countries.

Although *Thich Nhat Hanh's* current fame in the Americas and Europe is as a Zen meditation teacher who leads spiritual retreats, his vocation as monk and peace activist began in Vietnam during the waning days of French colonialism, World War II, and the Vietnam War. Receiving full monastic ordination in 1949, he founded the An Quang Institute of Buddhist Studies in Saigon in 1950, and Van Hanh Buddhist University and the School of Youth for Social Service in the mid-1960s. The latter became one of the primary centers of socially engaged Buddhist activism dedicated to healing the violence of the Vietnam War on the streets of Saigon. In 1966, Nhat Hahn presented a five-point peace proposal to Washington that included a timeline for U.S. troop withdrawal, and in 1969 he headed the Vietnamese Buddhist Peace Delegation during the Paris Peace talks. After the end of the Vietnam War, he helped organize rescue missions for Vietnamese refugees trying to escape from political oppression.

In 1965, Nhat Hanh founded the Order of Interbeing (Tiep Hien) headquartered at the Plum Village Monastery in the south of France with other centers in Europe and North America based on the fundamental principle that peace in the creation of human communities requires not merely political, economic, and social change but inner transformation. A prolific writer and widely sought-after speaker, Nhat Hanh continues his activities as a peace advocate including peace marches at MacArthur Park, Los Angeles, in 2005 and 2007. He teaches the essential relationship between contemplation and action; that the realization of one's deepest, spiritual self and active involvement on behalf of the well-being of others are interdependent; and that the cultural transformation necessary for the development of just, harmonious communities goes hand in hand with the practice of mindful awareness.

After he returned to Thailand in 1961 having completed university and law degrees in Wales and England, *Sulak Sivaraksa* became a major force in developing intellectual concern over the social, economic, and political problems facing Thailand and creating a series of NGOs to address them. They have included the Coordinating Group for Religion and Society (CGRS), an ecumenical Buddhist and Christian human rights organization; the Thai Inter-religious Commission for Development (TICD) that has sought to encourage Buddhist student associations to participate in social service and social change programs, to act as a bridge between rural and urban sectors of society, and to promote educational projects for children in slum areas; and the Santi (Peace), Pracha (Democratic) Institute (SPDI). The SPDI's projects include the Thai Forum Program that provides information to the mass media on alternative approaches to peace and justice; the Thai-Indochinese Dialogue Project that facilitates dialogue among Thai, Lao, Khmer, and Vietnamese; and Sekiyadhamma, an organization that assists and supports the work of monks dedicated to developing a constructive Buddhist challenge to the rapid destruction of the natural environment and the dissolution of religious and cultural values.

S. Sivaraksa articulates his philosophy of social and political activism in terms of a creative reinterpretation of traditional Buddhist teachings. For example, he extends the moral precept not to take the life of a sentient being to the use of chemical fertilizers and insecticides that deplete the soil of rich microorganisms, the destruction of forests that contributes to the loss of biodiversity, and the contamination caused by the dumping of nuclear and chemical waste. He directs the moral precept against lying toward a critique of advertising that promotes excessive consumption and prurient sensationalism in news reporting; and for S. Sivaraksa the Buddhist principle of non-attachment becomes an attack on consumerism, corporate greed and unjust economic systems that exacerbate the gap between the rich and the poor, and the commoditization of culture.

One of the most active groups working for peace in Sri Lanka has been the Sarvodaya Shramadana movement (Awakening of All Through the Gift of Labor). It was founded by *A.T. Ariyaratne* in 1958 as a rural self-help program that over the years has organized Shramadana development programs in over eight thousand villages. The programs are based on the basic Buddhist principles of sharing (*dana*), constructive activity (*arthacharya*), and equality (*samanathamatha*) and seek to promote individual and community material and spiritual harmony and well-being. Sarvodaya has grown into the largest welfare organization in the island with 1,500 full-time employees and approximately 200,000 volunteers. It cares for over 1,000 orphaned and destitute children and sponsors 4,335 preschools that serve over 98,000 children. With the escalation of the conflict between the Sinhalese dominated government and the Tamil minority in 1983, Ariyaratna increasingly turned his efforts toward peace building. These activities included setting up the first camps for Tamil refugees, organizing peace conferences, leading peace marches, organizing relief programs in conflict areas, and initiating a fund to aid the people of the Northern Province affected by displacement.

Inspired by both Buddhist teachings and Gandhian ideals, Ariyaratne's vision aims at a reform of the values and structures that create conflict. With that goal in mind he directs a Buddhist critique at political and economic structures in Sri Lanka with the goal of challenging partisan party politics and consumerism. Currently, he contends, Sri Lanka party politics are dominated by: *chanda* (alienation based on caste, linguistic, racial, and communal divisions used by political parties to promote self-interest rather than the well-being of all); *dvesha* (political propaganda based on rumor and falsehood that promotes violent confrontation); and *bhaya* (a spirit of fear and mutual suspicion promoted by a handful of politically powerful people for their own personal benefit). Likewise, the economy fails to serve the needs of all classes but, rather, promotes the material well-being of a small minority and is rife with corruption. Buddhist economics, by contrast, seeks increased efficiency in production (*uttarasampada*), protection of natural resources and the environment (*arakkasampada*), a cooperative rather than competitive social ethos (*kalayamittata*), and a wholesome, sustainable lifestyle (*samajivakata*) for all. Ariyaratne appeals primarily to Buddhist principles, although he reinterprets them in inclusive, ecumenical terms that challenge social and political barriers and highlight the common spiritual values shared by temple, kovil, mosque, and church.

In 1966, *Dharma Master Cheng Yen*, a Taiwanese nun, founded the Buddhist Compassion Relief Tzu Chi Foundation. It has become one of the largest non-profit philanthropic organizations in the world with a staff of over five hundred and 30,000 trained volunteers with headquarters in Taiwan and branches in over thirty countries. The Buddhist Tzu Chi Foundation opened a California branch in 1989 and currently has over 100,000 members. Specializing in poverty alleviation, medical care, vocational training, environmental protection, and disaster relief, the Foundation built its first hospital in eastern Taiwan in 1986. Since then, it has opened five more hospitals, a college of medicine (1994) that has become Tzu Chi University, and in 1989 founded Taiwan's first private nursing college.

The Foundation has supported numerous disaster relief projects around the world including responding to the devastation caused by the 1996 typhoon and 1999 earthquake in Taiwan, and sending 3,000 volunteers to Banda Aceh and 1,000 to Sri Lanka in the wake of the 2004 Tsunami. Given Dharma Master Cheng Yen's strong service orientation, it is not surprising that she often appeals to the Buddhist principles of love, compassion, sympathetic joy, and equanimity, and the Bodhisattva idea symbolized by Guanyin. In response to the devastating earthquake in Haiti the Foundation organized a relief effort that included 400,000 packs of instant rice, 30 tons of cornmeal, 50,000 blankets, 10,000 boxes of bottled water, 150,000 anti-inflammatories, 5,000 body bags, and other canned food and medical supplies. The effort was promoted under such banners as "Walking the Path of Compassion," and "Gathering the Love of All to Care for Quake Survivors in Haiti."

No generalization adequately characterizes the historical and contemporary record of the world's religions regarding the perennial, if not intractable, challenges of world peace, institutional violence, economic injustice, and systemic intolerance. For example, although the principle of non-violence (*ahimsa*) figures prominently in Buddhist ethics, violence has been part of the Buddhist historical record, and Buddhist communities today are not exempt for intolerance and internal conflict. However, as illustrated by the international prominence of H.H. Dalai Lama, the life and work of Thich Nhat Hanh, Sulak Sivaraksa, A. T. Ariyaratne, Dharma Master Cheng Yen, and many others, it is beyond dispute that Buddhist leaders throughout the world are seriously engaged in "creating a culture of peace and justice for the entire human community" that address political conflict, economic injustice, civil rights, and human welfare through the creation of new institutional structures, reinterpreting Buddhist teachings, and reallocating material resources to meet the global challenges of the 21st century.

CROSSCURRENTS

RELIGION, WORLD ORDER, AND PEACE
Jewishness and Global Justice*

Jeff Israel

"Religion, World Order, and Peace" should focus the attention of religious and spiritual leaders on the contributions they can make to peace-building. As I read it, the paper makes two especially compelling suggestions: religious and spiritual leaders should engage in vigilant self-criticism and they should develop practical peace-building techniques. Applied to the topics of special concern listed at the end of the paper (treatment of minorities, conflicting interpretations of religious freedom, etc.), I believe such efforts will indeed promote peace among religious people. At the same time, I have concerns about the prominent role of religion and religious leadership in global politics envisioned by the authors. I gather from language used in the paper that they are well aware of the kinds of concerns I have in mind. To this extent, some of what follows is an elaboration on issues already implicitly identified by the authors.

In my short reflection I will, first, express some particular concerns about how Jews fit into a world order where religious leaders enjoy special political recognition. Second, I will express some related but more general concerns about the role of religious leadership in a just world order. Finally, I will conclude by portraying a vision that significantly overlaps with that of "Religion, World Order, and Peace" and joins the effort of its authors to harness the full diversity of human communities and traditions in the pursuit of global justice.

*See especially, Azza Karam, "Concluding Thoughts on Religion and the United Nations: Redesigning the Culture of Development," pp. 462–474, in this issue.

A variety of organizations and individuals ostensibly represent Jews in global politics. Let us look at three cases that involve the United Nations and peace-building. Many Rabbis have been involved in interreligious initiatives to build a global consensus for peace. The Millennium World Peace Summit of Religious and Spiritual Leaders held in the hall of the United Nations General Assembly is a good example. Rabbis have also signed declarations, engaged in dialogues, and joined Christian and Muslim clergy on other occasions hoping specifically to inspire an end to conflicts in the Middle East. When Rabbis engage in interreligious peace-building, they are seated next to priests, ministers, imams, etc., as professional clergy that minister to people of the Jewish faith. In these contexts, they function either as representatives of particular communities (if they are Chief Rabbis or congregational Rabbis) or as interpreters of concepts like peace and justice in the religion of Judaism, or as both.

Alternatively, consider the Conference of Presidents of Major American Jewish Organizations. The Conference of Presidents communicates Jewish interests to political leaders around the world and supports efforts at the United Nations to counter anti-Semitism, condemn terrorism, and undertake institutional reform. To be sure, some of its member organizations are rabbinical organizations. But it is not a religious organization and its leaders are certainly not religious leaders. I would describe it, instead, as an umbrella organization tasked to coordinate unified Jewish responses to pressing Jewish concerns. A prominent way that the Conference of Presidents seeks to contribute to peace is by defending the State of Israel from political attacks in the global public sphere that it perceives to be threatening and unjust.

Of course, the State of Israel has its own mission to the United Nations. Israel's mission to the UN is involved in humanitarian, economic, cultural, and political activities like the missions of other member states. The policies and initiatives of the Israeli delegation reflect those of the current governing party or coalition in Israel, which is elected through democratic procedures. It is often directly involved in peace negotiations that include the United States, European countries, the Palestinian Authority, Egypt, Jordan, and others.

So, Jews are recognized in many ways on the global political stage and are engaged in as many kinds of peace-building. While the authors of "Religion, World Order, and Peace" do not endorse official representation of religions at the United Nations, their vision of a "new spirit of public responsibility" does seem to include an increasingly prominent platform at the UN for religious leaders (at events like the Millennium Peace Summit of Religious and Spiritual Leaders, for instance). This will be a welcome invitation to prominence for those Jewish leaders that represent Jews primarily as adherents to the "world religion" of Judaism in interreligious politics.[1]

But this is only one of several competing ways to represent the Jews. I would say, for instance, that the Conference of Presidents reflects a picture of the Jewish people as a transnational ethnic polity with the State of Israel as its national homeland. On the other hand, the State of Israel can be seen as an ethnically diverse democratic state that has a distinctive Jewish history, character, and language but has ultimately supplanted "Jews" with "Israelis" as the relevant category for global politics. (There are, of course, many ways to see the State of Israel.)

In everyday life, these prominent pictures of Jewishness often blur together or overlap without seeming to strain Jewish self-perception. But they are actually quite different from one another and, depending on the circumstances, entail different prospects for future Jewish life. My own view of Jewishness is compatible with some of the prominent views, but it is a distinct alternative: I prefer to describe Jews as a network of families linked by a chain of texts, events, ideas, symbols, rituals, and memories anchored in the Hebrew community of ancient Judea.[2] Our given names are *Am Yisrael*, and *B'nai Yisrael*, and there are others. We are *sui generis*, one of a kind.

Wherever Jews are compelled to describe or explain the chain of relations that binds us together, we are thereby compelled to undertake a political act of translation. This means that we must fit ourselves into a recognizable political category: we must make ourselves politically visible. Over millennia, we have found it expedient to be recognized as an *ethnos*, a religion, as *dhimmis*, a *Volk*, nation, culture, etc.[3] Among the results are Rabbis that function as professional clergy,[4] organizations like the Conference of Presidents, and the State of Israel.

Most Jews that represent these approaches do so with sincere *Ahavas Yisroyal* (love of *Am Yisrael*); I am in solidarity with all of them on this basis, even if we disagree about the translation of Jewishness into political categories. And, to be sure, undeniable advantages come with the prominent contemporary approaches. Religions can demand tolerance, accommodation, and free exercise (and participate *as religions* in public life). Ethnic groups can demand national self-determination and cultural survival. States can provide safety and security for their citizens and guarantee their rights (and contribute to global justice as members of organizations like the UN).

My view does not lead to any such political opportunities. Not posited as a religion among religions, or an ethnicity among ethnicities, or a nation among nations, Jews, in my view, are left invisible to politics. And politics is rendered remote from Jewishness: being Jewish, in and of itself, proffers no justifications for any political claims. On the other hand, I think my view captures more vividly Jewish life as it is actually lived and leaves open the most and best possibilities for future Jewish life.[5]

For example, there are many Jews who are cut off from the sources of thriving Jewish life because they have been convinced that to be Jewish is to be "religious." Since these Jews would never see or describe themselves as "religious," they find themselves alienated from their own Jewishness, stifled, stunted, and unable to thrive as Jews. Jewish self-perception according to my view of Jewishness is meant to help Jews work-through such neuroses. It is meant to free Jews from the constraints of one-dimensional political categories; it is a view of full flourishing, finally, for Jews.[6]

From my particular Jewish perspective, then, I am concerned that the increased recognition of religious leaders as principal actors in global politics envisioned by the authors of "Religion, World Order, and Peace" will further privilege the specifically *religious* picture of Jewishness *among Jews*. I will call this "the *religionizing* effect": the process by which people are incentivized to define themselves narrowly by an answer to the question "what is my religion?"[7] When a respected global political institution like the United Nations sets its honorific gaze on a particular kind of group leadership, the effect is to bolster the authority of just these sorts of leaders (by contrast to their competitors). Compounded by the establishment of the category of religion in most national constitutions, such international recognition of religious authority will undoubtedly contribute to the "Medusa Syndrome" that already too often petrifies organic Jewish life into religion.[8]

But it is not only the inadvertent *religionizing* effect on Jewishness that concerns me when I consider a higher profile for religious leaders in global politics. I also worry that there will be a further *religionizing* effect on persistent conflicts, and the parties involved in these conflicts, that will actually get in the way of their just resolution. In order to explain myself, I think it will be helpful to stipulate a distinction between peace and justice as political terms. Let us say that peace is the absence of intrusive violence and chaos. And let us say that justice is the presence of stable institutions that guarantee to each and every person what he or she is owed by virtue of being a person. Given these stipulative definitions, I am happy to say that religious leaders, like other kinds of community leaders, can indeed contribute greatly to peace. But I assume that people around the world (including, of course, Jewish people) must rely on the institutions of territorially defined states to establish and maintain justice.

Furthermore, I assume that what each and every person is owed by virtue of being a person corresponds roughly to the kinds of rights enumerated in the Universal Declaration of Human Rights: the right to express oneself freely, the right to assemble, the right to choose one's political representatives, the right to own property, etc.[9] And I assume that, at least as a practical matter, states with centralized governments and clear borders are the best political entities for guaranteeing these rights. I will call a state that *genuinely* guarantees basic rights to all of the people within its borders: a just state.[10] A just world order is one organized into just states.

Finally, I assume that all people (including, of course, Jewish people) are best able to thrive in the myriad idiosyncratic, indefinable, and ever-changing ways that people want to thrive, when they live in just states.[11] So, from a Jewish perspective (according to which I want Jews to be able to thrive freely) and from a political perspective[12] (according to which I want all kinds of people to be able to thrive freely) I passionately endorse a world order of strong states working with each other—through organizations like the United Nations[13]—to be just. In this vision of a just world order, each and every person, finally, has a chance to flourish.[14]

I worry that the prominent inclusion of religious leaders in peacebuilding at the UN (and in other such high-profile contexts) might undermine the efforts of states to define local conflicts in terms of injustice and to resolve such conflicts by establishing justice.[15] The Israeli–Palestinian conflict can serve as an example. The most salient fact about this conflict, from the perspective of justice that I have described above, is the fact that Palestinians in Gaza and the West Bank do not live within the borders of a clearly defined state. Progress toward justice requires either that the State of Israel take full responsibility for the persons living in both Israel proper and the Palestinian territories *under one state* or that a Palestinian state is established so that the responsibility for guaranteeing justice is *split between two states*.[16] Thus, on my account, the most important work to do in order to resolve this conflict and establish genuine prospects for sustainable justice is the work of *state*-building.

Unfortunately, there are religious leaders on both sides of this conflict who insist on framing the conflict in narrowly religious terms and get in the way of the pragmatic state-building necessary to promote justice. From my perspective, such individuals should not be given a platform for their views at the UN. And they should certainly not be included simply on the basis of their claims to religious authority. On the other hand, to the extent that prominent religious leaders want to help promote the development of just states to govern the people living in Israel and the Palestinian territories (or anywhere else), they should be welcome on the global political stage.

The point is that a claim to religious authority is not really a relevant criterion for inclusion as a "leader" in global efforts to promote justice. Actually, I assume that religious leaders can contribute no more or less, on balance, than prominent union representatives, business executives, local politicians, tribal heads, celebrities from television and film, artists, musicians, novelists, athletes, journalists, editorialists, historians, philosophers, and others. Indeed, I suspect that the cause of justice would be advanced more successfully if *all* of these types of prominent people (from Israeli society and Palestinian society, and from those around the world admired by Israelis and Palestinians) would gather in the hall of the United Nations General Assembly to declare their support for a just resolution to the conflict.[17]

Since I do believe it is important to mobilize non-state actors on behalf of global justice, I would like to suggest that the relevant criteria for inclusion are *community leadership* and *significant public admiration*.

Obviously, I have a lot of work to do to explain my use of these terms. For now, I will propose that a community leader is someone that a group of people actually relies on in identifiable ways to represent them and give them guidance; a significantly admired individual is someone that is critically and popularly recognized for excellence in a major sphere of human life. There are *many* religious leaders who meet these criteria and they should be mobilized to promote global justice on this basis.

I suspect that the authors of "Religion, World Order, and Peace" are aware of the concerns that have led me to suggest these more general criteria. I imagine that similar concerns led them always to refer to "religious *and spiritual* leaders" and to refer to "different traditions, worldviews, and patterns of belief." It seems fair to assume that they too are loath to impose artificial categories that can stifle people's otherwise dynamic lives and get in the way of justice. My approach is meant to go farther in this direction. It allows for the inclusion of the relevant religious people in global efforts to pursue justice without inadvertently imposing a *religionizing* effect on Jews, Palestinians, or any other people or conflicts.

Notes

1. On the idea of "world religions" see: Tomoko Masuzawa, *The Invention of World Religions* (Chicago: The University of Chicago Press, 2005). For a concise history of the meaning of the term "religion" see: Jonathan Z. Smith, "Religion, Religions, Religious," in *Relating Religion: Essays in the Study of Religion* (Chicago: The University of Chicago Press, 2004), 179-196.
2. The ancestral Jewish community, on my account, lived in Judea in roughly the sixth and fifth centuries B.C.E. It was composed of Judeans who returned from exile and those that never left after the destruction of the First Temple in Jerusalem, and perhaps some non-Judeans that threw their lot in with the Jews. This is the community that built the Second Temple in Jerusalem, redacted the textual core of Jewish life, and was, most importantly, linked by a chain of texts, events, ideas, symbols, rituals, and memories to the families of Abraham, Isaac, and Jacob (whose stories are recounted in the Torah and Midrash).
3. A good place to start reading about Jewish self-definition in relation to prevailing political categories and constraints is: Shaye J. D. Cohen, *The Beginnings of Jewishness: Boundaries, Varieties, Uncertainties* (Los Angeles: University of California Press, 1999).
4. On the transformation of Rabbis into "clergy" see: Ismar Schorsch, "Emancipation and the Crisis of Religious Authority: The Emergence of the Modern Rabbinate," in *From Text to Context: The Turn to History in Modern Judaism* (Hanover, NH: Brandeis University Press, 9-50. And: Michael A. Meyer, *Response to Modernity: A History of the Reform Movement in Judaism* (New York: Oxford University Press, 1988), esp. 100-142.

5. Intellectually, my view of Jewishness has been shaped by readings of Jewish thinkers like Franz Rosenzweig, Martin Buber, Ahad Ha'Am, Simon Dubnow, and Micah Joseph Berdichevski. Rosenzweig wrote in 1920, for instance, "All recipes, whether Zionist, orthodox, or liberal, produce caricatures of men, that become more ridiculous the more closely the recipe is followed." Franz Rosenzweig, "Towards a Renaissance of Jewish Learning," in *On Jewish Learning* (New York: Schocken Books, 1965), 66. He also lamented any further revival of "that old song, already played to death a hundred years ago, about Judaism as a 'religion,' as a 'creed,' the old expedient of a century that tried to analyze the unity of the Jewish individual tidily into a 'religion' for several hundred rabbis and a 'creed' for several tens of thousands of respectable citizens... God keep us from putting that old cracked record on again..." Ibid. 57.

6. I am moved by Berdichevski when he writes, "Our hearts, ardent for life, sense that the resurrection of Israel depends on a revolution—the Jews must come first, before Judaism—the living man, before the legacy of his ancestors"; Berdichevski knew well that "Israel precedes the Torah." Micah Joseph Berdichevski, "Wrecking and Building" [c. 1903], in *The Zionist Idea*, edited by Arthur Hertzberg (Atheneum, NY: The Jewish Publication Society, 1959), 294.

7. For a sophisticated and much broader look at how this process works, see Olivier Roy's discussion of "deculturation" in *Globalized Islam: The Search for a New Ummah* (New York: Columbia University Press, 2004).

8. Anthony Appiah describes the "Medusa Syndrome" in his book *The Ethics of Identity*, where he writes: "in the realm of identity there is no bright line between recognition and imposition." Kwame Anthony Appiah, *The Ethics of Identity* (Princeton, NJ: Princeton University Press), 110. For an account of how the dynamics described by the "Medusa Syndrome" function in the American legal context see: Winnifred Fallers Sullivan, *The Impossibility of Religious Freedom* (Princeton, NJ: Princeton University Press, 2005).

9. I think the clearest account of precisely what should be guaranteed by states can be made in terms of "central human capabilities"; I have not used this language, which is less familiar than "rights," so as to avoid confusion. For more on the Capabilities Approach and its relation to human rights, see: Martha C. Nussbaum, *Frontiers of Justice: Disability, Nationality, Species Membership* (Cambridge: The Belknap Press of Harvard University Press, 2006).

10. It is not enough for rights to be guaranteed on paper by a state constitution; all of the people within the borders of a just state must *actually* be able to have the kinds of flourishing lives that guaranteed rights allow. See, again, Nussbaum, *Frontiers of Justice*. On how one might measure the justice of a society using the Capabilities Approach, see: Jonathan Wolff and Avner de-Shalit, *Disadvantage* (New York: Oxford University Press, 2007).

11. It is worth noting that Article 18 of the Universal Declaration of Human Rights ascribes to human beings the right to "freedom of thought, conscience, and religion." Clumping religion with thought and conscience may helpfully avoid the *religionizing* effect on Jews and others: it implies that a person may have strong convictions, beliefs, attachments, etc., which must be protected but are not understood by that person to be "religious." Then again, a state constitution may be able to catch all of the rights we care about with the freedom of expression, freedom of assembly, and freedom of conscience without referring to "religion" at all.

12. On the "political perspective," see: Charles Larmore, *Patterns of Moral Complexity* (Cambridge: Cambridge University Press, 1987), and John Rawls, *Political Liberalism* (New York: Columbia University Press, 1996).

13. I must report, here, that there seems to be widespread distrust of the United Nations among Jews. I have on many occasions read and heard accusations of anti-Semitism at the UN in Jewish publications and in conversations with other Jews. As I understand it, anti-Semitism is the political ideology that organizes politics around a conflict between malevolent Jewish interlopers and the good people whom they exploit, corrupt, or otherwise harm. [See: Norman Cohen, *Warrant for Genocide: The Myth of the Jewish World Conspiracy and the Protocols of the Elders of Zion* (London: Serif, 1996); Stephen Eric Bronner, *A Rumor About the Jews: Antisemitism, Conspiracy, and the Protocols of Zion* (Oxford: Oxford University Press, 2003); and *The Book of Esther* 3:8-14.] Antisemitism can be compared to other conflict ideologies like Marxism (the ideology that organizes politics around a conflict between workers and owners of the means of production) or Fanonism (the ideology that organizes politics around a conflict between colonizers and colonized). Accusations of anti-Semitism have been made recently about: UN General Assembly resolutions on Israel, activities at the World Conference Against Racism in Durban in 2001, and the Goldstone Report on the invasion of Gaza in 2009. There is not space for me to evaluate these accusations here. But I can say: global justice is incompatible with anti-Semitism. So, I trust that the United Nations, which was founded on the defeat of Nazi anti-Semitism, will continue its pursuit of global justice by vigilantly opposing anti-Semitism wherever it emerges.

14. To be clear, my political aspiration for all kinds of people to be given a chance to flourish is subject to moral constraints: if a person's "flourishing" will cause injustice it should be prevented in a just state.

15. In this respect, I find the inclusion of religious leaders that claim *transnational* authority especially worrisome: the interests of such individuals may be far removed from the practical establishment of justice for people embroiled in complex local conflicts.

16. According to my view of justice it is also necessary for Palestinians to enjoy full basic rights equal to those of their neighbors in the states where they already live (including Israel, Lebanon, Jordan, and Syria).

17. I agree with Amartya Sen when he writes: "The recognition of multiple identities and of the world beyond religious affiliations, even for very religious people, can possibly make some difference in the troubled world in which we live." *Identity and Violence: The Illusion of Destiny* (New York: W. W. Norton & Company, 2007), 79.

CROSSCURRENTS

RELIGION, WORLD ORDER, AND PEACE
Christianity, War, and Peacemaking

James Heft[1]

All religions need to examine how they contribute to the common good, which includes more people than those who follow a particular religion. The United Nations Secretary General's recent invitation to all religious and spiritual leaders to examine how they contribute to creating a culture of justice and peace for the world community provides an ideal opportunity for that examination. A central part of that culture for Christians is their attitudes toward war and peacemaking. Those attitudes have evolved dramatically over time, especially in the last century.

Christianity has gone through many changes with regard to war and peacemaking, beginning with the first few centuries when Christians refused to join Rome's Imperial Army, to the first elaborations of the Just War doctrines beginning in the third century, to the Crusades in the medieval period, and to the present day when the largest single group of Christians, Roman Catholics, officially have made the criteria for a just war more difficult to meet than ever and have begun to elaborate the requirements for peacemaking. Among themselves, however, the world's over two billion Christians continue to disagree on these matters, with some groups supporting preemptive military actions and others pacifism.

Historically speaking, the position of Christians in the world has no doubt affected their understanding of the morality of war and peacemaking. The New Testament texts themselves never directly address the morality of war, although the example of Jesus, especially as he faced his own death, suggests a strong non-violent attitude. The earliest Christians, a small minority tucked into the seams of the huge Roman Empire, could adopt (without much notice) a pacifist position. But with the passage of time, however, Christians entered the military, and religious leaders were forced to reflect more systematically on the morality of armed conflict. Once Christianity had become the official religion of the Roman Empire, Augustine (354–430) elaborated a theory about when war could be "justified" morally: namely as a response of love to a neighbor who has been threatened by force.

Thomas Aquinas (1225–1274) developed the idea of the "just war" further by legitimating self-defense as a reason for war. Throughout the Middle Ages, however, popes themselves not only called for the Crusades to reclaim the Holy Land from the Muslims, but also did not hesitate to use force to protect their interests and to enforce their policies. It was not until the papacy was forcibly stripped of the papal states by Italian nationalists in 1870 that the pope's exercise of power shifted dramatically to the moral and spiritual dimensions of leadership. Pope Benedict XV (1914–1922) tried unsuccessfully to end World War I and to create an international alliance among the nations of the world. In 1944, a year before President Truman approved the use of the atomic bomb over Japan, an influential Jesuit moral theologian published an article that condemned saturation bombing.

Pope John XXIII (1958–1963) initiated a richer and broader vision of war and peacemaking when he reiterated in a fresh and compelling way the need for an international body with responsibility for defining and defending human rights. Just two years after Pope John's death, his successor, Pope Paul VI (1963–1978) spoke before the United Nations and cried out, "No more war, war never again!" One of the documents of Vatican II (1962–1965) flatly condemned total war and called for political leaders, indeed all people of good will, to approach war with a totally new attitude; that text (*Gaudium et spes*) also endorsed non-violent resistance. In later encyclicals, Pope Paul identified the work for justice as the basis for a lasting peace. From 1870 to 1978, therefore, a profound shift had begun to take place in the Catholic teaching about war and peacemaking.

More than any other pope in modern history, Pope John Paul II (1978–2005) reshaped the Catholic Church's understanding of the just war theory. As first and foremost a social philosopher, Pope John Paul II based his rethinking of "Just War" on his understanding of the freedom and dignity of the human person, the centrality of human rights, and the promotion of non-violent methods to bring about political and social change. For this pope, the centrality of the human person led him to focus on the person of Jesus, especially as he suffered on the cross. He believed that anyone who entered deeply into the sufferings of Jesus would be in a better position than someone standing in the *Realpolitik* school "to discern the often narrow path between the cowardice which gives in to evil and the violence which, under the illusion of fighting evil, only makes it worse." More and more, after the Gulf War of 1991, the pope spoke of the importance of non-violent means and the demands of peacemaking. While never a pacifist, this pope, toward the end of his papacy, promoted a theology of peacemaking of which the theory of the just war is only a part. Increasingly after the genocide in Rwanda, he spoke in favor of the use of force for humanitarian interventions. Perhaps the clearest expression of John Paul II's transformation of the traditional just war doctrine is his 2002 World Day of Peace Message, "No Peace without Justice, No Justice without Forgiveness." In preparation for the Year 2000, he repeatedly confessed the sins of the Church over the centuries, including "the use of violence in the service of truth."

It is most likely that John Paul II's own acute awareness of the devastating consequences of war made him even more cautious to endorse the traditional just war theory. Instead, he began to emphasize what a number of ethicists have recently drawn attention to: not just to the *jus ad bellum* (legitimate reasons for the use of force) and to the *jus in bello* (how to conduct a war morally), but also to the *jus post bellum* (the obligation to forgive and rebuild after a war).

Benedict XVI (2005–) has repeatedly insisted on religious freedom. He has also defended the separation of Church and State, but not of religion from society. In other words, religion should be free to influence, not control, public policy. Despite mistakenly quoting in a 2006 address a medieval ruler who denigrated Mohammad, Benedict strongly argued that religion and violence should have nothing to do with each other. So strongly has he spoken about the importance of the protection of the environment, that he has been dubbed the "green pope."

Finally, in accord with papal teaching, the American bishops have consistently called for universal health care coverage (including undocumented immigrants), the reform of insurance companies that deny coverage to people with preexisting illnesses, and an end to abortion.

Many mainline Protestant churches have supported the direction taken by John Paul II. In contrast, fundamentalist and some evangelical Christians have backed much less restrictive limits on the traditional just war theory, especially when it comes to a military defense of Israel and, in general, opposition to Muslims, whom many conservative Christians believe follow a false religion. The small but increasingly influential pacifist Christians (for example, Church of the Brethren, the Mennonites and, after the example of pacifist Dorothy Day, Catholics) continue to oppose all use of force. For their inspiration, pacifists from the beginning drew upon the example of Jesus; on the other hand, Roman Catholics thinkers, especially John Paul II, returned to the example of Jesus, especially once they grasped the devastating consequences of modern warfare. Roman Catholics, then, especially when they follow the leadership of John Paul II, have moved more and more to emphasizes not the use for force, but rather the need for non-violent methods, peacemaking and justice, the only lasting basis for peace.

I have great hope now that much of Christianity can contribute, as it always should have, to creating a culture of justice and peace for the world.

Note

1. James L. Heft, S.M. is Alton Brooks Professor of Religion at the University of Southern California and President of the Institute for Advanced Catholic Studies.

CROSSCURRENTS

RELIGION, WORLD ORDER, AND PEACE
A Muslim Perspective

Abdulaziz Sachedina

David Little's piece on "Religion, World Order, and Peace," has underscored the importance of engagement with religious communities and their leaders in making the international order more peaceful and free of intolerance and violence. His essay has identified several topics of special concern with the purpose of garnering the active support of religious communities whose traditions are open to all sorts of retrieval by different interest groups within a single normative tradition to either further or stifle the positive role religion can play in public sphere. In the following pages, I will endeavor to address specific issues that need to be raised in the context of Islamic tradition and its political/public goals that need to be reformulated to accommodate the reality of not only the plurality of religions but also intrafaith relations that seek justification in the normative sources of Islam, such as the Qur'an and the Tradition (Sunna). Based on my field experience in the Muslim world, I will also focus on the importance of the need for the UN to connect to religious leaders in Muslim nation-states and not just their autocratic rulers. Relevant in this connection is the public–private issue as navigated by an Islamic understanding of pluralism and consensual politics and the UN's need to get religiously literate to influence the course of events in the Muslim world to promote freedoms of religion and expression as the fundamental human rights of all citizens. Obviously, the latter goal cannot be achieved without holding accountable those who continue to rule with force and violence even when they lack the necessary political legitimacy.

Since 9/11, the world of the faithful in Muslim societies has been in turmoil because the living Islam, dominated by its traditional interpreters, the learned ulema, has not been able to guide the community at the most critical period of its existence. As indicated by Little, it is not only "flawed" religion that can become the breeding ground for violence and conflict; it is also the unjust politics that becomes the source of a violent posture adopted by religiously sensitive people to combat their corrupt leaders. To say that Islam is a peaceful religion that has been hijacked by a few militant extremist is to mislead the world to its internal tensions generated by different versions of Islamic ideals—from those versions advocating peaceful coexistence to those urging full conquest of the world for God's religion. Likewise, there is a range of views within Islam about appropriate responses to undemocratic governance in the Muslim countries.

The internal dialogue among Muslims has as yet to confront the real questions about Islam's spiritual and moral potentials that could be harnessed by the national governments and an international body like the UN to bring about peaceful resolution to ongoing conflicts in many parts of the Muslim world. A real partnership between the UN and Muslim religious leadership that may hold a key to unlock those interpretations of Islam that can further peace has not as yet been realized. The acute problem that the international body faces is its inability to garner the support of the influential religious leaders who could act as conduit to the goals that were articulated on the occasion of the Millennium World Peace Summit of Religious and Spiritual Leaders in the year 2000. I am sure that the question: "Who speaks for Islam and Muslim communities?" has been on the mind of many organizers at the UN. With the lack of political freedom in most of the Muslim countries where human rights violation occur more frequently, the UN needs to seek other ways of implementing incremental progress in people's right to consensual politics. This is the key to correct many areas of concern in Little's "topics of special concern." The two areas of special concern, in my opinion, are as follows: first, the need for the UN to identify influential spiritual/moral leadership in the Muslim world, who are also deeply committed to the reinterpretation of the Islamic normative sources and their implementation in advancing democratic governance with a commitment to uphold international conventions on human rights; and second, the need to dialogue with the militant Muslim leadership to placate their suspicion of the international body that is perceived as the enemy of Muslim people in their unflinching support of the autocratic rulers who have shown very little interest in defending their citizens' fundamental human rights.

The most important issue raised by Little's essay is the need to change the way religious communities have thus far been passive as peacemakers. A concerted effort on the part of international community needs to be made to encourage religious and spiritual leaders to engage in self-criticism of their tradition and to reallocate spiritual and moral resources in transformation of those sacred teachings that are prone to abuse and destruction of all bridges of understanding among the people. Historically, there has not been any better time than the 21st century for religious communities to do more than pay lip service to human dignity as the sole criterion for respect and tolerance of the cultural and religious "other." Globalization of the world economy has led to the intense search for some stronger bond than the existing systems of international relations assumed under the world body like the UN. Even the moral commitment to the Universal Declaration of Human Rights has fallen short in promoting the rights of religious or ethnic minorities who continue to labor under various forms of discrimination under national governments. In some ways, it is the communitarian interpretation of a religious tradition that has provided sanctions for the majority Muslim governments to continue to stifle all endeavors toward improving the human rights of all citizens. Obviously, the UN has not considered its essential role to involve bringing the main players—both political and religious—to the table to further a better understanding within a militant Muslim leadership and those Muslim governments whose claim to political legitimacy is challenged by their own citizens.

A broader understanding of Muslim political culture is needed to garner the support of Muslim people to various forms of democratic participation. This is a key element in getting traditional Islam to become a partner to universal notions of democracy, pluralism, and human rights. Muslim political culture has been informed by certain religious beliefs about political participation that tends to rationalize or legitimize the existing order. There is a correlation between religious and cultural aspects of this problem in Muslim societies. These aspects have influenced the ways in which Muslims have conceived of their political space and their participation in them. And, although the Muslim world has increasingly blurred the line between religion and politics, it is my contention that some sort of functional secularity has always predominated in negotiations about political space independent of religious presuppositions about its management. Contrary to the views held by a number political analysts, the terminology of the classical legal tradition of the Shari'a is not very helpful in nurturing norms and values that would enhance more peaceful international relations or the advancement of a consensual politics within majority Muslim societies.

In the Islamic context, as the UN needs to take into consideration, even under the influence of modernization and secularization, political participation on the part of Muslims is shaped by what Muslims understand of their public role and responsibilities in the light of their religious identity. In Islamic juridical tradition, Muslims have a duty to acknowledge the lawfully established authority within the category of the religious obligations imposed by the Shari'a. Among both the Sunni and the Shi'ite communities, political quietism or a policy of quiescence and acceptance of existing circumstances until a qualified leader could establish an ideal Islamic polity was regarded as a political strategy to avoid the greater evil of chaos in the society. The question of justice, however subjective and contingent upon different points of view that both the leaders and the people bring to bear upon their understanding of human condition, informs Muslim political culture in its context-dependent political strategies. To account intelligibly for the ways in which Islamic tradition continues to influence people's reactions to a culture that is dominated by repressive politics and total absence of observable participation of the people in the state's political processes, we need to discover the guidelines about legitimate political behavior in Islamic religious thought. The latter provide a context that reveals the way militant groups negotiate their political space with sensitivity toward their religious beliefs. Their political choices under repressive political systems include religiously sanctioned political activity that sustains a public order that is not necessarily religious and yet regarded as necessary for the well-being of its membership.

Although Little has advocated a more sensitive approach to religion's public role in modern society, he has not addressed the tendency in modern political discourse with its secularist universalistic appeal to devalue communitarian identities founded upon collective religious constraints and sanctions that provide necessary social environment for practical connections between individuals and groups. Communitarian identities are in competition with the contemporary liberal politics that absolutizes individual moral agency by freeing individual from collective restraints that are needed for smooth functioning of political order. This is the core problem in the acceptance of religious claims as having legitimate place in public forum. The secular political discourse is based on the so-called public versus private distinction that would place religious commitments and grounds for action in a sphere isolated from that of public discourse and public choice. At stake is the place of various religious considerations in both public discussions about political activity, ranging from individual Muslims on religious grounds publicly condemning such acts as homosexuality or collective Muslim denial of women's right to marry outside the community in accordance with the religious duties in the Shari'a. A public discourse claims to have an integrity of its own and requires Muslim community to abide by a neutrality required of the secular public order to maintain peace and harmony in society. This secular demand for public discourse is founded on the premise of universal reason that actually excludes making moral and metaphysical claims bearing on political choices in terms understandable only in the context of religious guidance embedded in the Qur'an and the Tradition. Traditional Muslim leaders, who exercise enormous influence in the public sphere, have a problem with the position that rejects the right of the people to decide political questions by what they regard as the best reasons rooted in a transcendent sphere of Islamic scriptures. The issue of proper public discourse and choice is of concern for all religious communities who must share a public forum with other religious groups, without insisting on the idea of whole truth connected with their own truth claims. It is in this connection that the religious perspectives of Muslim traditionalists become critical to explore. In the absence of the ecclesiastical authority mediating between God and humanity in all those acts that one performs as part of one's relationship to the transcendent, Muslim religion defines the communal context to include only interhuman relationship. In this manner, Islamic public discourse defines itself by leaving individual autonomy within its religiously based public order by leaving individual free to negotiate his/her spiritual destiny without state interference, while requiring his/her to abide by the public order that involved the play of reciprocity and autonomy upon which a regime of claims and entitlements is based. The emphasis on individual bound by duties does not negate the notion of individual possessing freedom to act in his/her own interest in the context of communal existence. In fact, it is important to underscore plurality in the estimation of human personhood and its relation to community. Indeed, this plurality exists not only in Islam, but also exists within different interpretations of secularism about individual's relation to one's religious commitments and community and to overarching secularized public sphere in the modern nation-state. It is for this reason that it may prove useful to inquire into the Islamic idiom for a different way of framing the terms of human valuation and worth, one that will allow mediation between public and private desiderata not always articulated as legitimate political activity.

The problem with individual political action informed by religious commitments and desiderata is the potential for the entanglement of these commitments with public discourse and public choice that affect other individuals, whether religious or not. There are certainly boundaries in the public sphere that must be recognized, without insisting that others agree with particular choices made, individually or in a group, on the basis of their religious reasons that necessarily apply to only those who have declared their commitment to abide its dicta. Thus far, the attitude of hostility, intolerance, and militancy against those who reject a particular response to the political issues has been the main source of conflict in Muslim societies. There is something in the public theology of Islam that can mitigate this hostile attitude by clearly demonstrating the classical heritage that recognizes the existence of a private realm separate from the public one to allow for ethical pluralism to determine interhuman relationship without diminishing the role of religious commitments in developing a social democratic constitutional polity.

Looking back to the last decade since the UN encouraged the world peace summit of religious and spiritual leaders, despite halting progression toward improving the standards of democratic governance in the

Muslim world, it is important to keep the momentum to build bridges of cooperation between secular institutions like the world body and religious and spiritual leadership for the betterment of humanity. Without the backbreaking efforts to garner the support of Muslim traditionalist leadership, usually suppressed by the Muslim governments and, consequently, off the radar of the UN organizers of important summits like the one on the occasion of the Millennium, the world should expect to face the militant solutions offered by frustrated Muslim extremists that have resulted in nothing less than destruction of innocent human life.

CROSSCURRENTS

SRI CHINMOY'S WORK AT THE UNITED NATIONS
Spirituality and the Power of Silence

Kusumita P. Pedersen

Introduction

Many may think of the United Nations mainly as the secular arena of political strife, but the World Organization has a spiritual dimension which, although it is often not visible to the general public, is intrinsic to its purposes. This essay describes the work of the philosopher, poet, humanitarian, and peace-server Sri Chinmoy (1931-2007) at the United Nations, a work that was devoted to bringing to the fore, fostering and articulating this spiritual dimension. Sri Chinmoy saw the United Nations not merely as a political institution but as "the Heart-Home of the World-Body" and the focal point of an emerging "world-oneness." For the United Nations to develop to maturity and to fulfill its divinely intended mission, he believed, its inner reality must be recognized and must function in concert with its outer reality. The responsibility to develop this approach belongs to the whole human community, but especially to those working directly for the UN and in association with it through non-governmental organizations (NGOs) or in other ways. This essay explores the significance of Sri Chinmoy's work in the perspective of a larger question: how do spirituality and meditation play a role in the overall context of the United Nations?

Invited by Secretary-General U Thant, Sri Chinmoy led regular meditations for peace at UN headquarters for thirty-seven years, beginning six years after he came to New York from his native India. He also conducted an array of other programs sponsored by Sri Chinmoy: The Peace Meditation at the United Nations, which was founded in 1970 to support the mission of the United Nations and promote the values expressed in its Charter. The Peace Meditation consists of United Nations staff members, delegates, journalists accredited to the UN, and representatives of NGOs; it is thus both internal to the United Nations structure and also open to participation from outside it. Sri Chinmoy's work beyond the United Nations through the Sri Chinmoy Centre, an international NGO, since its inception in 1966 has advocated peace based on spiritual values, rooted in meditation and expressed in music, art, poetry, sports, community service, and celebration of the achievements of people from all cultures and backgrounds. A worldwide network of three hundred Sri Chinmoy Centres and their collaborating groups carries on the innovative programs founded by him, with no charge to participants. These include humanitarian aid in over one hundred and twenty-five countries, at times in partnership with UN agencies, and the World Harmony Run, a global torch relay for friendship between peoples involving hundreds of thousands of participants in more than one hundred countries, with its opening and closing ceremonies at UN headquarters and the UN Office in Geneva. A single, indivisible vision of peace and human transformation informs all of these activities, whether organized by the Peace Meditation at the United Nations or undertaken elsewhere under NGO auspices.

In the fall of 2007 in a spacious conference chamber at the United Nations Secretariat, representatives of Buddhism, Christianity, Hinduism, Indigenous religions, Islam and Judaism stood together without speaking a single word to open Sri Chinmoy's memorial service. This interfaith invocation was perceptibly longer than the usual "moment of silence" and recalled the non-sectarian meditations he had led twice every week year after year. One of the most compelling features of those meetings was their silence. The deep stillness might include a musical interlude, but there would be almost no speaking. Sri Chinmoy gave many lectures at the United Nations and engaged in informal discussions responding to questions, while the Peace Meditation has held a wide variety of programs, but all this is distinct from the meditation itself. The power of silence in meditation was and continues to be the foundation of all the work initiated by Sri Chinmoy. Its premise is that spirituality—an inner life connecting us to a larger or deeper reality—is a capacity possessed by every person. All people, regardless of religious and cultural background or institutional location, can and should apply this capacity in their efforts towards the goal of peace.

The Secular, the religious, and the spiritual at the United Nations

Officially, the United Nations is secular. At its founding, Member States included a number of countries with Communist governments adhering to an atheist ideology and some others possibly resistant to the use of religious language. Since approval by Member States was needed, the founding documents, the United Nations Charter of 1945 and the Universal Declaration of Human Rights of 1948, make no mention of God and set forth no religious doctrine in a narrow or conventional sense. At the same time, the very purpose of the United Nations as stated in these documents is to bring about world peace, establish justice, affirm the dignity of the human person and ensure that all people live together in tolerance and peace as good neighbors. The ringing words that begin the Preamble to the Charter are as follows: "We the peoples of the United Nations, determined to save succeeding generations from the scourge of war, which twice in our lifetime has brought untold sorrow to mankind, and to reaffirm faith in fundamental human rights, in the dignity and worth of the human person, in the equal rights of men and women and of nations large and small." The Preamble to the Universal Declaration holds up the same goals of "freedom, justice and peace in the world," makes human dignity a fundamental principle and refers to "the human family."[1]

The ideals of peace and justice and the vision of the oneness of humankind do not originate with the United Nations. Even as some elements of the founding documents are new, these themes are ancient and central to the ethics of the world's religious traditions. Ethics in turn is integral to these traditions and is not separable from their religious character. The explicit ethical universalism of the United Nations documents and their affirmation of the unity of the human are arguably themselves religious ideas, while phrases such as "made in the image of God," "all under heaven" or "the world is one family" (which were familiar to the drafters of the documents, a number of whom were deeply versed in their own religions)[2] can be said to hover between the lines as an implicit reference to the sacred and the transcendent. The United Nations has relied on the non-governmental sector, and on Religious NGOs specifically, to deal with the explicitly and particularly religious aspects of society. The spiritual dimension, however, is pan-human. It is the element that not only transcends the divisions between religions,[3] but also cannot be easily confined to one kind of institution or another.

The United Nations in the context of spiritual evolution
In his affirmation of its inner reality, Sri Chinmoy views the United Nations as the outcome of an age-long journey of cosmic progress in which evolution is spiritual as well as physical. In his lectures and talks given at the United Nations, as well as throughout his other writings in poetry and prose, he gives an account of how the divine reality which is immanent in creation through involution gradually comes forth, or evolves. In this process God's qualities of light, peace, joy, and beauty are over time received and assimilated by the world in the transformation Sri Chinmoy calls "God-manifestation," which culminates in perfection. Born in East Bengal and growing up during twenty years on the Sri Aurobindo Ashram, Sri Chinmoy shares this evolutionary vision with Swami Vivekananda and Sri Aurobindo, one of whose major works is *The Ideal of Human Unity*.[4]

In the process of spiritual evolution, it is with human beings that a conscious longing for global oneness appears for the first time.[5] Within this vaster picture of human destiny, Sri Chinmoy identifies the United Nations as crucially important for the achievement of the goal of human unification and world harmony after thousands of years of war and struggles for domination. The United Nations is the established and concrete outcome of the dream that brought the League of Nations into temporary existence earlier in the twentieth century.

> The United Nations is an instrument, a significant instrument of God for His searching, aspiring and loving humanity. This instrument is the Joy of the Creator and, at the same time, the joy of the creation. The United Nations embodies both Heaven's Vision and earth's reality. There was a time when Heaven's Vision was only partially manifested as reality. We called it the League of

Nations. Then, the League of Nations was transformed into reality, and it became the United Nations.[6]

The League of Nations was a dream-seed.
The United Nations is a reality-plant.
The aspiring and serving life of man's universal oneness will be the Eternity-Tree.[7]

Sri Chinmoy declares, "The United Nations is not merely an organisation ... Rather, it is the way, the way of oneness, that leads us to the supreme Oneness."[8] The very fact that its goal is universal peace signals the key role of the United Nations in God's plan for the world: "To me, the United Nations is divine," Sri Chinmoy says. "Why? Because it is the fond child of the Supreme dedicated to promoting world peace."[9] This is peace in its fullest sense: "Peace does not mean the absence of war ... Peace means the presence of harmony, love, satisfaction and oneness. Peace means a flood of love in the world family. Peace means the unity of the universal heart and the oneness of the universal soul."[10]

Sri Chinmoy states that appreciation of the importance of the United Nations cannot rest on perception of externals but rather should be based on understanding of its real nature as an essential part of God's dream for the progress of humanity. He reminds us that the organization is young and "time is a great factor."[11] Our view of the United Nations should be aspirational: "We cannot judge the United Nations on its present achievements. We cannot judge the United Nations by what it has already offered us. We can only judge the United Nations on its soulful promise, its promise that it will one day flood the world with boundless peace."[12] He adds, "It is very easy to criticise an organisation. But an organisation is composed of human beings, and humans are still far, far from perfection."[13] Moreover, what the United Nations is able to achieve outwardly depends on the acceptance of its founding vision, with its inherent spiritual dimension, by human beings—that is, each of us—and our dedication to ensuring that this vision becomes a reality. Because of this, Sri Chinmoy tirelessly calls for recognition of the inner or spiritual reality of the United Nations. He says,

> Our source is peace and our manifestation is bliss on earth. If we know what we are and what we stand for, then the United Nations can become for us the answer to world-suffering, world-disharmony and world-ignorance. The inner vision of the United Nations is a gift supreme. This vision the world can deny for twenty, thirty or even a hundred years [or for centuries]. But a day will dawn when the vision of the United Nations will save the world. When the reality of the United Nations starts bearing fruit, then the breath of Immortality will be a living reality on earth.[14]

He fervently exhorts, "The Compassion of God has been unceasingly descending upon the United Nations. Now it is up to the world."[15]

The role of meditation at the United Nations
For all of these reasons, Sri Chinmoy holds that "Prayer and meditation are of supreme importance if we are to manifest the inner role of the United Nations."[16] He begins a talk entitled "Does Meditation Really Accomplish Anything?" with the response, "Is there anything that meditation cannot accomplish?"[17] The precedence of the spiritual is based on its capacity to illumine the outer world. In silence, it is possible to go beyond the senses, the ordinary emotions and the mind, and to access the enlightened knowledge, serenity, strength and compassion of the heart and of the soul, which is a representative of the Divine.[18] As Sri Chinmoy explains, "[I]f we become one with the inner reality, which is our silence-life, which is God's Vision, then we can bring it to the fore and transform the outer reality."[19] Silence is therefore the key to genuine progress. Sri Chinmoy did not view this message as bringing to the United Nations something new or adventitious, but rather as unfolding from within what is already there and is urgently needed. The inner reality, with its boundless power for good, is available to us if we will only pay attention to it and embrace it. Denying that "spirituality is only for the chosen few," Sri Chinmoy stresses that "The art of meditation is something inherent in each individual."[20] While his lectures at the United Nations are often highly philosophical, they deal as well with all aspects of spirituality as it is actually lived. Sri Chinmoy also spent considerable time in discussion with UN delegates, diplomats, staff members and NGO representatives about the practical aspects of

meditation and ways to undertake their daily work as a service to humanity.²¹

In emphasizing silent meditation as a regular part of life at the United Nations, Sri Chinmoy consciously built on the legacy of some of its early leaders. The summit values of universal peace and humanity's oneness were made part of the United Nations at its creation, as we have seen. Following this, acknowledgment in custom and practice of its spiritual dimension goes back almost to its beginnings. In 1949, a rule was put in place to open and close each year's General Assembly session by observing "one minute of silence dedicated to prayer or meditation."²² It is important to note that even at this early stage, an NGO played a key role in catalyzing the integration of a spiritual aspect into the United Nations proper. This was the Laymen's Movement for a Christian World, which was founded in 1941 and included prominent American businessmen among its members. Its Executive Director, Weyman C. Huckabee, had advocated the minute of silence, and also successfully urged that a Meditation Room be created within the UN. The original Meditation Room was established by the first UN Secretary-General, Trygve Lie, when the UN was still located at its interim headquarters in Lake Success on Long Island.²³

Dag Hammarskjöld and U Thant

Dag Hammarskjöld, the second Secretary-General, is the author of a famous posthumously published journal of his spiritual life, *Markings*.²⁴ Less is heard about his active role in supporting and personally designing the Meditation Room in the public lobby of the UN. The permanent Meditation Room opened in 1952, two years after the headquarters building itself. In 1957, Hammarskjöld wrote about its meaning:

> We all have within us a center of stillness surrounded by silence. This house, dedicated to work and debate in the service of peace, should have one room dedicated to silence in the outward sense and stillness in the inner sense. It has been the aim to create in this small room, a place where the doors may be open to the infinite lands of thought and prayer. People of many faiths will meet here,

and for that reason the room is empty of familiar religious symbols. A giant block of iron ore placed at the center of room and illuminated by a single beam of light evokes "the meeting of the light, the sky, and the earth . . . it is an altar to the God of all."[25] Hammarkjöld saw a spirituality embodied in silence as the inner center of the United Nations. This spirituality is not restricted to any particular religion but is common to all religions. Remarkably, there are people living thousands of miles from New York who have never visited the UN but are aware that the Meditation Room exists and think of it as a sign of the fuller meaning and purpose of the United Nations. While many admittedly take a more skeptical view, there are some who see the United Nations as an archetype of human oneness and an embodiment of the hope for peace, in the conviction that the United Nations is not just an outer, political entity but something more.

Saying that "The United Nations needs completely self-sacrificing and self-giving servers"[26] Sri Chinmoy holds up as paradigmatic the lives of Dag Hammarskjöld and his successor, U Thant. Both, even while holding the highest office in the United Nations, exemplified the complete integration of spiritual life with service to the world community in the spirit of self-offering. On Dag Hammarskjöld, Sri Chinmoy says, "He was a seeker of the highest order. His heart cried for the satisfaction of mankind. His mind cried for the illumination of mankind...He became the fulfilling bridge between humanity's excruciating pangs and Divinity's illumining Compassion."[27]

U Thant succeeded Dag Hammarskjöld as Secretary-General in 1961 after Hammarskjöld died in a plane crash outside the then Northern Rhodesian town of Ndola. Thant was a devout Buddhist from Myanmar and a lifelong and daily practitioner of meditation. He was convinced that spiritual and ethical values common to all religions must be the foundation of the work of the United Nations. In his farewell speech to UN staff members, given in 1971, he sums up his views. It is worth quoting at length.

> I have certain priorities in regard to virtues and human values. An ideal man, or an ideal woman, is one who is endowed with four attributes, four qualities—physical, intellectual, moral and spiritual qualities. Of course it is very rare to find a human being who is endowed with all these qualities but, as far as priorities are concerned, I would attach greater importance to intellectual qualities

over physical qualities. I would attach still greater importance to moral qualities over intellectual qualities. It is far from my intention to denigrate intellectualism, but I would attach greater importance to moral qualities or moral virtues over intellectual virtues—moral qualities like love, compassion, understanding, tolerance, the philosophy of "live and let live," the ability to understand the other person's point of view, which are the key to all great religions. And above all, I would attach the greatest importance to spiritual values, spiritual qualities. I deliberately avoid using the term "religion." I have in mind the spiritual virtues, faith in oneself, the purity of one's inner self which to me is the greatest virtue of all. With this approach, with this philosophy, with this concept alone, will we be able to fashion the kind of society we want, the society which was envisaged by the founding fathers of the United Nations.[28]

U Thant personally supported Sri Chinmoy's meditations for peace and other initiatives at the United Nations. His daughter Aye Aye Thant, now president of the U Thant Institute, recalls, "Sri Chinmoy's life represented the best thought, most far-reaching vision and outstanding artistic and practical accomplishments. It was my father's and Sri Chinmoy's shared vision for world peace based on the ideals of tolerance and compassion that had brought mutual respect and admiration between them."[29] In 1972, Sri Chinmoy dedicated his play on the life of the Buddha to U Thant, who with his family attended a special premiere performance.[30] After U Thant's passing in 1974, the Peace Meditation inaugurated the U Thant Peace Award to honor his memory. Its recipients over the years have included President Mikhail Gorbachev, President Nelson Mandela, and Mother Teresa. Among his many tributes to U Thant, Sri Chinmoy has said, "Sincerity spoke through him, integrity breathed in him, spirituality walked with him. He knew the world-problem: ignorance. He knew the world-answer: meditation, and this he practiced in silence."[31]

Programs of the Peace Meditation at the United Nations
U Thant had wanted the United Nations to be from time to time a place where the world's religions would meet for dialogue.[32] Sri Chinmoy was

a deeply committed supporter of the global interfaith movement and the Peace Meditation at the United Nations in the early 1970s sponsored what may be some of the first interfaith programs at the UN. Interfaith prayer services observing the National Day of Prayer were held beginning in 1975. The Peace Meditation has collaborated with the Center for World Thanksgiving and organized interfaith Peace Walks, as well as observances of the anniversary of the Meditation Room and a well-attended annual Interfaith Prayer Breakfast, hosted each year by one of the Permanent Missions with that country's Ambassador presiding. Sri Chinmoy on a number of occasions offered an opening silent meditation at such events as the fifth Spiritual Summit Conference of The Temple of Understanding, held in New York and at the UN in 1975, and the annual Interfaith Service in New York observing the opening of the UN General Assembly, begun in 1997. For the Parliament of the World's Religions, he offered the opening meditation at the centenary Parliament in Chicago in 1993 and again in Barcelona in 2004. Interfaith events and non-sectarian silent meditation can be seen as complementary, the one specifically interreligious and the other transreligious.

The Peace Meditation since its launch in 1970 has also offered a wide variety of other programs as well at UN headquarters, including lectures, panel discussions, commemorations, inspirational symbolic events, and cultural events of all kinds, often highlighting the traditions of Member States. Meditations for peace are also conducted at the United Nations Office in Geneva. Over the years, the Sri Chinmoy Centre NGO has held UN-related events in cities around the world, such as observances of United Nations Day and athletic events dedicated to peace.

Conclusion
The pioneering work of Sri Chinmoy, along with that of many members of the United Nations community and its affiliated NGOs, has over time contributed to a growing consensus on the essential role of spirituality in the mission of the UN. Many now make a commitment to the integration of a spiritual, values-centered and interfaith perspective into work on critical global issues and partnership-building. There is greater freedom than there was thirty years ago to speak about this perspective and on appropriate occasions to engage in prayer and meditation. Important examples, among others, of this direction are the formation of the NGO

Committee on Spirituality, Values and Global Concerns,[33] a member of the Conference of NGOs in Consultative Status with the United Nations (CONGO) as well as of the less formal Spirituality Caucus. To say that outer peace depends on inner peace may have been considered naive in the past, but today this familiar statement seems like common sense and a necessary operating principle. "Political will" is frequently mentioned as indispensable for change, and will, after all, is a matter of motivation and consciousness—an inner or spiritual entity. Similarly, "world oneness" can be seen as the spiritual, and also positive, aspect of globalization. Oneness is not sameness or homogeneity, but a form of community that affirms diversity along with those things that unite us as human beings. Sri Chinmoy has said that "Unity can be achieved through manifested multiplicity,"[34] and "A nation is a limb of the universal body. Each limb is necessary, essential and indispensable. Each nation represents humanity's hope, humanity's promise and humanity's progress in a unique way."[35]

How can Sri Chinmoy's vision be further manifested and its realization in practice grow and increase its positive contributions? First, there is the question of how reality is seen, or of worldview, which can determine or influence much of our actions. Sri Chinmoy understands the United Nations and its purpose in an immense evolutionary context and in terms of an integral view of the human person that places great stress on inner experience as well as outer action. For members of Religious NGOs and others who belong to a faith tradition, such a view may resonate strongly with convictions already held. Some others may find it sufficient to see the universalist ethics of the founding documents of the United Nations as the expression of a global, egalitarian spirituality that can inspire and guide a life of service, as Sri Chinmoy advocates. For everyone, it is helpful to have regular, frequent occasions on which to remember and reflect in various ways upon the founding vision of the United Nations, to inquire into its profound meaning and also to celebrate and receive inspiration.

The practice of meditation and prayer is of paramount importance, as we have seen, because of its transformative capacity. Sri Chinmoy compares the release of the power of silence to splitting the atom, and declares, "Silent meditation is the strongest force that can ever be seen, felt and utilized."[36] The union of meditation with self-offering action is the ideal, as exemplified by Dag Hammarskjöld and U Thant. Such a practice provides insight and skill for effectiveness, patience and strength to endure, and above all the widest and deepest view of what one is trying to do and for what reasons. Sri Chinmoy stresses that meditation is not for one's own individual benefit alone and quotes Hammarsjköld's saying, "No peace which is not peace for all."[37] The silence of meditation holds within itself the power to bring about a world of universal peace, but for this power to contribute concretely to the work of the United Nations and of Religious NGOs, it must be acknowledged, valued, and actually used by an ever-increasing number of people who aspire for world-oneness.

Notes

1. The United Nations Charter is available at http://www.un.org/en/documents/charter, while the Universal Declaration of Human Rights can be found at http://www.un.org/en/documents/udhr/index.shtml and is widely available elsewhere.
2. See Mary Ann Glendon, *A World Made New: Eleanor Roosevelt and the Universal Declaration of Human Rights* (New York: Random House, 2001).
3. See Kusumita P. Pedersen, "Spirituality beyond the Boundaries of Religion," *Current Dialogue* 47 (June 2006): 29-33.
4. Sri Aurobindo, *Social and Political Thought* (Pondicherry: Sri Aurobindo Ashram Trust, 1970). At the United Nations, this philosophy of spiritual evolution has resonated with those influenced by the thought of Pierre Teilhard de Chardin, including Assistant Secretary-General Robert Muller.
5. Sri Chinmoy, *The Garland of Nation-Souls: Complete Talks at the United Nations* (Deerfield Beach, Florida: Health Communications, 1995), 15. Hereafter *Garland*.
6. *Garland*, 15.
7. *Garland*, 27. Sri Chinmoy does not regard the League of Nations as a failure, since it was the parent or forerunner of the United Nations, which carries on the League's original inspiration. See *Garland*, 55.
8. *Garland*, 16.
9. *Garland*, 10.
10. Ibid.
11. Ibid.
12. *Garland*, 39.
13. *Garland*, 18.
14. *Garland*, 19.
15. *Garland*, 22.
16. *Garland*, 63.
17. *Garland*, 265.
18. It should be said here that the contemplative traditions in many religions offer practical teachings similar to this in their general outlines.

19. *Garland*, 18.
20. *Garland*, 96, 75.
21. See Sri Chinmoy, *Flame-Waves: Questions and Answers at the United Nations*, Parts 1-13 (New York: Agni Press, 1975-1978).
22. Rule 62 of the *Rules of Procedure of the General Assembly*. Available at http://www.un.org/ga/60/ga_rules.html
23. See "The UN Meditation Room: Prayer and Meditation at the United Nations," *Meditation at the United Nations* 5, No. 8 (August 1977): 6-33. This is the transcription of a program at Wainwright House in 1977 at which the Peace Meditation presented Mr. Huckabee with an award. On that occasion much of this history was recounted by those who had been directly involved.
24. Dag Hammarskjöld, *Markings*, translated by Leif Sjoberg and W. H. Auden, with a Foreword by W. H. Auden and a new Preface by Jimmy Carter (New York: Random House, 2006 [1963]).
25. http://www.un.org/Depts/dhl/dag/meditationroom.htm, retrieved February 15, 2010.
26. *Garland*, 48.
27. *Garland*, 43, 42.
28. U Thant, *United Nations Staff Committee Bulletin* 281 (28 December 1971): 7. I am indebted to Adhiratha Keefe for this reference.
29. *A Celebration of the Life of Sri Chinmoy, 1931-2007, Leader of Peace Meditations at the United Nations* (New York: Agni Press, 2007), 15.
30. Sri Chinmoy, *Siddhartha Becomes the Buddha* (New York: Agni Press, 1972). See also his *U Thant: Divinity's Smile, Humanity's Cry* (New York: Agni Press, 1977).
31. *Garland*, 46.
32. The author's notes of Aye Aye Thant's remarks at the Millennium World Peace Summit of Religious and Spiritual Leaders, held at the United Nations and the Waldorf-Astoria Hotel in New York, August 28-31, 2000.
33. For details see the Committee's website at http://www.csvgc-ny.org, which also contains "A History of Spirituality at the United Nations." I am indebted to Audrey Kitagawa for this reference.
34. *Garland*, 21.
35. *Garland*, 36.
36. *Garland*, 277, 252.
37. *Garland*, 265.

CROSSCURRENTS

THE SALVATION ARMY AND THE UNITED NATIONS—BEING GOOD NEIGHBORS

Carolyn J. R. Bailey

The United Nations signed its charter in 1945, at the end of World War II. It said, in part, that those involved with the United Nations "determined to save succeeding generations from the scourge of war, which twice in our lifetime brought untold sorrow to mankind." The Salvation Army was one of the original twelve NGOs, which became involved with the United Nations in 1947. It was a natural connection for The Salvation Army as an international movement. The Salvation Army had gone to war with the troops, meeting their needs at the front lines; it was active in various war-torn countries as responders to need; it had a history of quick responses and was known for being able to mobilize easily and well. From 1947 to the present, the length of involvement alone indicates sympathy of purpose.

In 2007, however, to further develop The Salvation Army's connection with the United Nations and to "prioritize the Army's involvement in international law, security, economic development, social progress, human rights and the achievement of world peace"—all areas in which the United Nations is active, General Shaw Clifton, the international head of The Salvation Army, opened the International Social Justice Commission (ISJC) in New York (*Caring*, p. 8). This makes it very clear that The Salvation Army understands its purposes, and the purposes of the United Nations are more than compatible and the relationship between the two groups is healthy and worth cultivating. Sympathetic and compatible, however, do not mean identical. In the next few pages, we will examine this relationship, what drives it and how it works. We will explore the various mandates involved—human, Christ's example, Scriptural, historical, and theological. We will also discuss the balance between the spiritual and the social work of The Salvation Army, which is always at the center of its own work and its work with other organizations.

Driven by the human mandate—being good neighbors
On the morning of December 26, 2004, a 9.0 magnitude earthquake, the most powerful in forty years, hit under the Indian Ocean, causing a tsunami, which killed tens of thousands of people in eleven countries and left untold damage in its wake. The Salvation Army was active in several of those countries, including Sri Lanka and India. In India, local Salvation Army officers (ministers) and soldiers (members) went to the areas of greatest damage, although those areas were outside their usual circle of influence. When The Salvation Army first arrived, the people in the community did not immediately embrace them. They were strangers from a different part of the country and from a different faith. But The Salvation Army had come to help its neighbors. In the immediate aftermath of the tsunami, The Salvation Army provided food, clothing, and temporary shelter. As time passed, The Salvation Army provided medical care and helped to rebuild homes. Most importantly, the people from The Salvation Army sat and listened to people's stories and helped them process their grief. When some other relief groups left, The Salvation Army stayed. Only then did the people trust that The Salvation Army really cared. Then they began to ask, "Tell us about this God of yours." This is the twofold mission of The Salvation Army, as indicated in its International Mission Statement: "to preach the gospel of Jesus Christ and to meet human needs in His name without discrimination."

The complete mission statement says, "The Salvation Army, an international movement, is an evangelical part of the universal Christian Church. Its message is based on the Bible. Its ministry is motivated by the love of God. Its mission is to preach the gospel of Jesus Christ and to meet human needs in His name without discrimination." It is this last part, "meeting human needs...without discrimination," which most closely connects the purposes of The Salvation Army with the purposes of the United Nations.

The purposes of the United Nations, as expressed in the Preamble to its Charter, are as follows: to work for world peace, to support fundamental human rights, to affirm the dignity and worth of the human person, and to work for the equal rights of men and women and of nations large and small, for justice, for social progress and for better standards of life for everyone. To achieve those ends, members commit "to practice tolerance and live together in peace with one another as good neighbours" (http://www.un.org/en/documents/charter).

What is the definition of a neighbor? Is it only those who live in close proximity to us? Is it only those with whom we feel an affinity?

This very question was raised in the tenth chapter of Luke when an expert in the law asked Jesus, "What must I do to inherit eternal life?" As He often did, Jesus answered with another question, "What is written in the Law? How do you read it?" The man answered, "Love the Lord your God with all your heart and with all your soul and with all your strength and with all your mind," and, "Love your neighbor as yourself." Jesus said, "You have answered correctly. Do this and you will live." But the expert wanted to justify himself, so he asked Jesus, "Who is my neighbor?" Jesus answered with the story of the Good Samaritan, a man who stopped to help a stranger, a man who might well have been his enemy, without counting the cost, because it needed to be done. When He finished the story, Jesus asked, "Which of these three do you think was a neighbor to the man who fell into the hands of robbers?" The expert in the law answered, "The one who had mercy on him." Jesus said, "Go, and do likewise."

In other words, we cannot say, "He is not my neighbor so I do not need to be concerned about what happens to him." Instead, we need to state the truth that, "Everyone is my neighbor so what happens to each person, matters."

This understanding is very similar to the Universal Declaration of Human Rights (December 10, 1948) which says (in part), "Whereas recognition of the inherent dignity and of the equal and inalienable rights of all members of the human family is the foundation of freedom, justice and peace in the world: All human beings are born free and equal in dignity and rights. They are endowed with reason and conscience and should act towards one another in a spirit of brotherhood (Article 1); everyone is entitled to all the rights and freedoms set forth in the

Declaration without distinction of any kind... (Article 2); everyone has the right to life, liberty, and security of person (Article 3); no one shall be held in slavery or servitude; slavery and the slave trade shall be prohibited in all their forms (Article 4); everyone has the right to a standard of living adequate for the health and well-being of himself and of his family (Article 25); and everyone has the right to education (Article 26)" (http://www.un.org/en/documents/udhr/index.shtml).

This might be called the "human mandate." We are humans together. There is no such thing as being more or less human, partly human, or almost human. A living being is human or it is not human. For that reason alone, because we are part of the same human family, we should care for each other. To continue the metaphor, because we are all neighbors on this planet, we need to look after each other. It is this human mandate that drives the United Nations. The Salvation Army also stands for the dignity of all human beings and works for peace and social justice.

In addition to this human mandate, however, The Salvation Army is driven by the mandate of Jesus Christ's example, a biblical mandate and a theological/historical mandate.

Driven by the mandate of Jesus Christ's example

Jesus Christ's example brings with it a mandate because of who The Salvation Army understands Him to be. The Salvation Army's fourth doctrine (statement of belief) says, "We believe that in the person of Jesus Christ the Divine and human natures are united, so that he is truly and properly God and truly and properly man" (Salvation Story, 1998). By coming as a man, Christ gave dignity to the human person and the human experience. As human, Jesus was body and soul, not just the divine in a temporary, unimportant shell. He was fully human, with human needs, and He knew what it was to be without. (See Matthew 8:19-20.) When people came to Him, He treated them as whole persons—body and soul, meeting their physical, emotional, and spiritual needs.

Jesus Christ was the full incarnation of God—God in the flesh, come to show us how to live. John 1:1 and 14 say, "In the beginning was the Word, and the Word was with God, and the Word was God... The Word became flesh and dwelt among us." *The Message*, a paraphrase by Eugene

Peterson, puts verse 14 this way: "The Word became flesh and moved into the neighborhood." This makes Jesus the ultimate good neighbor and gives those who seek to follow His example a challenge.

Why did Jesus "move into the neighborhood"? As told in Luke 4:16-21, after Jesus fasted in the desert for thirty days and was tempted by Satan, He went to Nazareth where He had been brought up. In the synagogue there, He opened the scroll to Isaiah 61 and read. This is the Scripture Christ used to declare His mission. Verses 1-3a say, "'The Spirit of the Sovereign Lord is on me, because the Lord has anointed me to preach good news to the poor. He has sent me to bind up the brokenhearted, to proclaim freedom for the captives and release from darkness for the prisoners, to proclaim the year of the Lord's favor.'... He began by saying to them, 'Today this scripture is fulfilled in your hearing.'" From the very beginning of His earthly ministry, Christ's heart is for the poor, brokenhearted, and captive.

Driven by a Biblical mandate

Christ Himself understood His actions were driven by a biblical mandate. The Salvation Army is also driven by this mandate. The first doctrine of The Salvation Army states, "We believe that the Scriptures of the Old and New Testaments were given by inspiration of God and that they only constitute the Divine rule of Christian faith and practice" (Salvation Story, 1998). In other words, The Bible is God's Word and Salvationists are compelled to do what it says. It says take care of the defenseless and do not oppress the vulnerable. There are three reasons to follow Scripture's clear directions: to avoid doom and judgment; to satisfy God's requirements; and to serve God Himself—being in right relationship with Him.

The Old Testament in particular has harsh words, words like doom and judgment, for those who mistreat the vulnerable. For example, Isaiah 10:1-3 (from *The Message* paraphrase) says, "Doom to you who legislate evil, who make laws that make victims—Laws that make misery for the poor, that rob my destitute people of dignity, exploiting defenseless widows, taking advantage of homeless children. What will you have to say on Judgment Day, when Doomsday arrives out of the blue?" Another Hebrew Bible prophet, Micah, said, "Doom to those who plot evil... They covet fields, and grab them. They find homes and take them. They bully the neighbor and his family, see people only for what they can get out of them...There will be no one to stand up for you, no one to speak for you before God and his jury" (*The Message*). From the book of wisdom, Proverbs, we hear, "You insult your Maker when you exploit the powerless" (14:31a, *The Message*).

The Bible does not only say, "Do not oppress the vulnerable." It also says, "Defend them. Take care of them." This is not a suggestion; it is a requirement. Micah 6:8 (NIV) says, "He has showed you, O man, what is good. And what does the Lord require of you? To act justly and to love mercy and to walk humbly with your God." In James 1:27 (NIV) it says, "Religion that God our Father accepts as pure and faultless is this: to look after the widows and orphans in their distress and to keep oneself from being polluted by the world." What is required? A heart that loves God moved to compassionate action on behalf of others. Isaiah 58:6-7 (NIV) puts it this way: "Is not this the kind of fasting I have chosen: to lose the chains of injustice and untie the cords of the yoke, to set the oppressed free and break every yoke? Is it not to share your food with the hungry and to provide the poor wanderer with shelter—when you see the naked, to clothe him, and not to turn away from your own flesh and blood?" (For more examples, see Exodus 22:22; Deuteronomy 10:18; Isaiah 1:17; Psalm 146:9; Psalm 68:5; Proverbs 25:21; and Isaiah 58:6, 7, 9a, 10).

Beyond avoiding doom or satisfying God's requirements, Scripture compels The Salvation Army to serve others as a natural expression of loving God and being in right relationship with Him. Service to others is service to God. This is beautifully described in Matthew 25:31-40 (NIV):

> When the Son of Man comes in his glory...all the nations will be gathered before him, and he will separate the people one from another . . . Then the King will say to those on his right, 'Come, you who are blessed by my Father, take your inheritance, the kingdom prepared for you since the creation of the world. For I was hungry and you gave me something to eat, I was thirsty and you gave me something to drink, I was a stranger and you invited me in, I needed clothes and you clothed me, I was sick and you looked after me, I was in prison and you came to visit me.'
>
> "Then the righteous will answer him, 'Lord, when did we see you hungry... thirsty... a stranger... needing clothes... or in prison'" and care for you?

"The King will reply, 'I tell you the truth, whatever you did for one of the least of these brothers of mine, you did for me.'"

The Salvation Army also serves in response to a theological and historical mandate.

Driven by a theological and historical mandate

The Salvation Army believes that God made humanity in His own image, as written in Genesis 1:26 and 27: God said, "Let us make man in our image, in our likeness..." So "God created (humanity) in his own image, in the image of God he created him; male and female he created them." As such, humans have inherent dignity and value.

God gave humanity free will, that is, the right to choose. Still, people chose to disobey God. God loves humanity so much that He wanted to bring about a reconciliation with humanity. God's plan is explained in John 3:16-17: "For God so loved the world that he gave his one and only Son, that whoever believes in him shall not perish but have eternal life. For God did not send his Son into the world to condemn the world, but to save the world through him." Jesus Christ lived to show humanity how, then died and rose again for everyone.

The Salvation Army's sixth doctrine states, "We believe that the Lord Jesus Christ has by his suffering and death made an atonement for the whole world so that whosoever will may be saved" (Salvation Story, 1998). There is no distinction, no arbitrary exclusion. Each person has the choice to accept the forgiveness or not. Those who accept God's forgiveness become part of the Church. The Church works to bring others back into relationship with God. This is as far as William Booth's early theology went.

William Booth, the founder of The Salvation Army, was a Methodist minister who wanted those who were overlooked, and unfortunately not always welcomed into the church, to know the saving grace of Jesus Christ. He did not intend to start a new denomination; he just wanted to be sure his neighbors heard the good news. But the Church as a whole was not ready to receive "the least of these." So William and Catherine Booth made a place where they were welcome.

The Salvation Army began in 1865 with one mission—to seek and to save the lost. As William Booth put it, "Go for souls and go for the worst." The Booths lived in Victorian England when one tenth of the population lived in abject poverty, lacking education, employment, and even basic necessities. Booth had a sense that very little could be performed about people's physical circumstances, so he was determined to give them hope of eternal salvation.

Once The Salvation Army had started, the Booths did not have a global vision for the work. Again, they wanted to bring the news of Jesus Christ's love to the people closest to them who were being overlooked. Yet within fifteen years, The Salvation Army had spread to six continents. Today, it is in 116 countries.

The Booths did not begin The Salvation Army with a vision for an integrated mission either, working with the entire person, body, and soul. As The Salvation Army spread, however, its work became as diverse as the countries in which it became established, meeting the very specific needs of the very specific people in each country. The beginning of The Salvation Army's organized social work was not in England, but in Australia, in 1883 with the establishment of a halfway home for released prisoners. William Booth began to realize the need for something more than his initial approach. He came to what he felt was a God-given understanding of what is sometimes called The Salvation Army's second mission. This was really the beginning of The Salvation Army's understanding of integrated mission.

It was William Booth's later theology which moved him, and therefore The Salvation Army, into its second mission—caring for humanity's physical, emotional and social needs as well as working for social justice. "(William Booth's) later theology of redemption still included personal salvation from sin for the individual who believes by faith; his later theology of redemption developed in such a way that it included social salvation from the evils that beset people in the world; and just as there was the possibility of universal spiritual redemption (i.e. salvation was not limited to the elect), so there was the possibility of universal social redemption. People were, however, responsible for either accepting or rejecting the offer of salvation" (Roger Green, Professor of Biblical and Theological Studies at Gordon College, in *Creed and Deed*, p. 62).

Of this development in Booth's theology grew his book, *In Darkest England and the Way Out*. It was a detailed scheme to assist what Booth called the "submerged tenth" of England's population—the poorest and most needy. At the beginning of *In Darkest England and the Way Out*, William Booth explained the Cab Horse's Charter—This was the living standard for the horses which pulled hansom cabs in London: "When he is down he is helped up, and while he lives he has food, shelter, and work." Booth was stunned that animals were treated better than human beings. He added, "That, although a humble standard, is at present unattainable by millions—literally by millions—of our fellow-men and women in this country" (Roger Green, *Creed and Deed*, pp. 66–67).

Long before, Dr. Abraham Maslow introduced the hierarchy of needs (physiologic, safety, social, esteem, self-actualization), William Booth came to understood that you had to meet physical needs before you could expect anyone to care about their spiritual needs. He expressed it this way: "But what is the use of preaching the Gospel to men whose whole attention is concentrated upon a mad, desperate struggle to keep themselves alive?" On another occasion he said, "Nobody gets a blessing if they have cold feet and nobody ever got saved while they had a toothache."

William Booth also said, "Our social operations are the natural outcome of Salvationism, or, I might say, of Christianity as instituted, described, proclaimed, and exemplified in the life, teaching, and sacrifice of Jesus Christ. Social work, in the spirit and practice which it has assumed with us, has harmonized with my own personal idea of true religion from the hour I promised obedience to the commands of God." Or, as it says in James 2:14-17 (NIV): "What good is it, my brothers, if a man claims to have faith but has no deeds? Can such faith save him? Suppose a brother or sister is without clothes and daily food. If one of you says to him, 'Go, I wish you well; keep warm and well fed,' but does nothing about his physical needs, what good is it?"

The Salvation Army, at its heart and at its best, cares for the marginalized, the overlooked, and the vulnerable through its integrated mission. Every Salvation Army soldier and every Salvation Army officer around the world to this day has promised to continue this integrated mission by signing "The Articles of War: A Soldier's Covenant." This includes the eleven doctrines and their application. The application includes "I will maintain Christian ideals in all my relationships with others, my family and neighbors, my colleagues and fellow Salvationists, those to whom and for whom I am responsible, and the wider community." Also, "I will be faithful to the purposes for which God raised up

The Salvation Army, sharing the good news of Jesus Christ, endeavoring to win others to Him, and in His name caring for the needy and the disadvantaged."

The United Nations and the Salvation Army's second mission

Taking good care of neighbors and caring for the needy and disadvantaged are two points at which The Salvation Army and the United Nations connect, have connected for the last fifty years, and will continue to connect. These connections are made at the local, national, and international levels. The Salvation Army's International Social Justice Commission (ISJC), while located in New York City, is actually under the auspices of The Salvation Army's International Headquarters (IHQ) located in London, England. At IHQ is the International Program Resources Department that supports The Salvation Army's development work around the world. Working closely with the International Program Resources Department is the office for international development in the United States, SAWSO (http://www.sawso.org). SAWSO, or The Salvation Army World Service Office, was established in 1978 and is located at The Salvation Army's National Headquarters in Alexandria, VA, just outside Washington, DC. Other countries have their own national offices. At the local levels, the ISJC encourages Salvation Army territories/commands around the world to link with regional UN offices.

It is commonly understood in the development world that faith-based organizations are excellent partners because they bring ready-made networks of people, and often facilities, to the table. This is true of The Salvation Army. As of the end of 2008, The Salvation Army has an active presence in 116 countries around the world. In developing countries, The Salvation Army currently has 50,000 indigenous officers (ordained ministers), employees and professional staff working (Salvation Army Year Book, 2008). These people, their communities, and the corps (TSA churches), schools, hospitals, rehabilitation centers, and other facilities in which they work, are natural networks for implementing new programs and services.

The ISJC fulfills its directive to build on The Salvation Army's participation in the UN, in part, by sending Salvation Army participants to UN-sponsored events on issues in which The Salvation Army is involved; by becoming more involved in the Council of Organizations; and, as has already been said, by encouraging territories/commands around the world to link with regional UN offices. The ISJC is The Salvation Army's principle international advocate and adviser on social, economic, and political issues and events that give rise to social justice in the world. Its stated purpose is to be "The Salvation Army's strategic voice to advocate for human dignity and social justice with the world's poor and oppressed." Its goals are "to raise strategic voices to advocate with the world's poor and oppressed; to be a recognized center of research and critical thinking on issues of global social justice; to collaborate with like-minded organizations to advance the global cause of social justice; to exercise leadership in determining social justice policies and practices of The Salvation Army; and to live the principles of justice and compassion and inspire others to do likewise."

The International Social Justice Commission also works with SAWSO. SAWSO's stated mission is "to support and strengthen The Salvation Army's efforts to work hand in hand with communities to improve the health, education, living, economic and spiritual conditions of the poor throughout the world." SAWSO works "to find long term solutions to poverty in less developed countries where The Salvation Army is active." SAWSO "works to help people help themselves through programs that improve living conditions, raise skill levels, increase productivity, and instill self-confidence." SAWSO understands that "community participation is critical if solutions are to be effective and enduring. In carrying out its programs, SAWSO's staff works through The Salvation Army's international network of facilities and personnel. SAWSO works with Salvation Army personnel and local leaders to identify the root causes of their problems, formulate solutions, and develop the skills necessary to plan and sustain programs in their communities. SAWSO also provides training in program planning and management, leadership, and community development."

A Chinese proverb, often quoted in development discussions, says, "Give a man a fish and he will eat for a day; teach a man to fish and he will eat for a lifetime." It is often used to show two ways of meeting human need as though they are mutually exclusive. They are in fact complementary. While it makes sense to teach a person to fish, the first question needs to be, is the individual starving or is his or her stomach full? If the stomach is full, go right ahead and begin the lesson. But if he or she is starving, there is a responsibility to provide fish. Then when there is an opportunity to focus on something other than immediate survival, one can give instructions on how to fish. This "relief to development" approach is the one most often used by The Salvation Army around the world.

Continuing its connection with the United Nations, The Salvation Army is addressing the Millennium Development Goals (MDGs) through its various programs. The Salvation Army is working to eradicate extreme poverty and hunger through WORTH[1] saving programs in Kenya, Tanzania, and Uganda; micro-credit programs in India, China, Zambia, Indonesia, and Sri Lanka; and food programs in Malawi, Uganda, and India. Achieving universal primary education is being addressed through schools and literacy programs in India, Uganda, Tanzania, Zimbabwe, Bolivia, Ecuador, Peru, Chile, Indonesia, Korea, China, Malaysia, and Singapore. Home Leagues in every developing country and anti-sex trafficking programs in China, Sri Lanka, Ecuador, and Eastern Europe promote gender equality and empower women. Community health programs in South Africa, Zambia, Zimbabwe, Congo DRC, Congo Brazzaville, Ghana, Bolivia, Ecuador, India, Indonesia, and Bangladesh work both to reduce child mortality and improve maternal health. A variety of programs in every territory in Africa, India, Indonesia, Bangladesh, Sri Lanka, China, South Korea, and Eastern Europe combat AIDS, malaria, and other diseases. Awareness, training, and fair trade programs are being set up to help establish a global partnership for development.

In addition to working toward meeting the MDGs, The Salvation Army participates on the following committees at the United Nations in Vienna, Geneva, and New York: the Commission on the Status of Women; the Commission on Crime Prevention and Criminal Justice; the Committee on Health; the Commission on Narcotic Drugs; the Committee on the Rights of the Child; the Committee on Spirituality, Values and Global Concerns; the Committee on the Working Group on Girls/International Network for Girls; the Ecumenical Women of the United Nations; the Ecumenical Working Group at the United Nations; and the Commission on the Status of Women.

The United Nations and the Salvation Army's first mission

This discussion of the long-term and continuing compatibility of the United Nations with The Salvation Army's second mission—social redemption—raises the question of the United Nations and The Salvation Army's first mission: individual redemption, or salvation. Before looking at The Salvation Army's relationship with the UN specifically, let's look at The Salvation Army's relationships with secular organizations in general.

To accomplish common goals, The Salvation Army often partners with secular organizations, i.e., organizations whose primary motivation is not faith based. Some of these organizations, many of them government based, put conditions on The Salvation Army's participation. Most often these conditions relate to curtailing what are considered the purely "religious" elements of Salvation Army programs. How can this be acceptable to The Salvation Army? As explained in *Hand in Hand: An Approach to the Integration of the Caring Ministries of The Salvation Army*, "The opportunity for a comprehensive ministry will be different in contracted programs from that in the usual programs of the corps. The Army engages in government and other contracted programs because it believes that meeting human needs and caring for hurting persons in the name of Jesus is a proper and desirable expression of the Gospel. It holds that such service, provided in a Christian manner, is of great value and is a spiritual ministry in its own right. Having accepted contractual constraints on its religious or denominational ministry, The Salvation Army still attempts to meet the total needs of all who come under the influence of its program."

It is perhaps ironic that The Salvation Army's relationship with the United Nations is not one of constraints. Individual governments and governmental organizations are often willing to accept The Salvation Army as an effective social organization but not as a church. One might surmise that the United Nations, a gathering of governments, would be exponentially restrictive. It is a case, however, of the whole being more tolerant than its parts. The UN understands, as does The Salvation Army, that to uphold and encourage human dignity and human rights, it must meet human need, without discrimination, in all its facets—political, social, economic, physical, and spiritual. Inherent in the UN Charter and the UDHR is the right to be one's true self, as individuals and as nations.

This includes religious expression. That means within the discussions of the United Nations, there is freedom and respect of religious expression. Lieutenant-Colonel Geanette Seymour represents The Salvation Army on the Global Women of Faith board. She says, "This is an opportunity for people of different faiths to come around the issue of peace; we all have a similar intent with different ways of accomplishing it." She continues, "People know that I am a Christian and expect me to be a Christian; they don't expect me to deny my faith. They treat me with dignity and respect, and ask for the same privilege from me" (*Caring*, p. 12).

The Salvation Army comes together with other groups for two main reasons. The first is to engage effectively and with reciprocity around issues, which matter to both groups. The second is to achieve a good outcome for the other group. For example, The Salvation Army might have a resource which would be useful to the group. Sometimes the connections are long lasting and sometimes they are brief. Sometimes, after an initial connection, a group chooses to go in a direction with which The Salvation Army is uncomfortable; a direction that is incompatible with who and what The Salvation Army is. In such cases, The Salvation Army chooses to part ways. As Lt.-Col. Geanette Seymour says, "We do not become something we are not."

As aforementioned, The Salvation Army does not get involved with other groups for the key purpose of turning those groups into Christian organizations. The Salvation Army does not engage with the United Nations with the intent of turning it into a Christian organization. The Salvation Army, however, is a church and will express itself as such. Its soldiers are Christians, and they will express themselves as such. For the most part, The Salvation Army finds that, when it participates with other groups, its Christian faith, expressed as grace and mercy and a willingness to go the extra mile, engenders hope. This makes it possible to engage around issues, like peace, HIV/AIDS and anti-trafficking. To deal with these issues, the whole of global society needs to become engaged with the solution. This is where partnerships such as the one between The Salvation Army and the United Nations become invaluable.

In whatever context The Salvation Army is working, under whatever constraints, it follows the command given in Colossians 3:17, which says, "And whatever you do, whether in word or deed, do it all in the name of the Lord Jesus, giving thanks to God the Father through him" (see also 1 Corinthians 10:31). Sometimes we are allowed to speak His name aloud, and sometimes we are not. That does not deter The Salvation Army because it has learned the lesson expressed in Luke 19:37-40. When Jesus entered Jerusalem on Palm Sunday, the week before His crucifixion, "the whole crowd of disciples began joyfully to praise God in loud voices for all the miracles they had seen: 'Blessed is the king who comes in the name of the Lord! Peace in heaven and glory in the highest!' Some of the Pharisees in the crowd said to Jesus, 'Teacher, rebuke your disciples!' 'I tell you,' he (Jesus) replied, 'if they keep quiet, the stones will cry out.'"

Conclusion

The Salvation Army has participated in the United Nations for more than fifty years and hopes to continue its involvement for the foreseeable future. Recent events make it clear that the world continues to need the concerted efforts of the United Nations and those NGOs which join in its mission to meet the needs of their neighbors without discrimination, and to work for peace and social justice. For example, on January 12, 2010, a 7.0 magnitude earthquake hit Haiti, devastating the island nation, which was still recovering from back-to-back hurricanes in 2008. Six weeks later, on February 27, 2010, an 8.8 magnitude earthquake hit Chile and was felt as far away as Sao Paulo, Brazil. Throughout Africa, HIV/AIDS continues its steady devastation. In far too many places, women and children are being sold and used as sex slaves.

William Booth could have been speaking for the United Nations when he said, "While women weep, as they do now, I'll fight. While children go hungry, as they do now, I'll fight. While men go to prison, in and out, in and out, as they do now, I'll fight. While there is a drunkard left, while there is a poor lost girl upon the street,...I'll fight." He made it a decidedly Salvation Army statement when he added, "while there remains one dark soul without the light of God, I'll fight, I'll fight to the very end."

Works cited

The Salvation Army, USA Western Territory, 2010, Caring: The Holistic Ministries of The Salvation Army. Volume 16, No. 1, Spring 2010. Long Beach, CA: New Frontier Publications.

Salvation Story: Salvationist Handbook of Doctrine, 1998. London: The Salvation Army International Headquarters.

Salvation Army Year Book, 2008. London: The Salvation Army International Headquarters.

Waldron, John D., ed. *Creed and Deed: Toward a Christian Theology of Social Services in The Salvation Army*. Canada and Bermuda: The Salvation Army, 1986.

Hand in Hand: An Approach to the Integration of the Caring Ministries of The Salvation Army. One of the Nationally Approved Publications

NIV/The Message Parallel Bible. Grand Rapids, MI: Zondervan, 2006.

Note

1. WORTH is an innovative women's empowerment program through which women teach themselves to read and write, become skilled in record keeping, generate personal and group savings, create successful small businesses, and become bankers in their own right.

CROSSCURRENTS

THE CENTER FOR INTERFAITH ACTION AND THE MDGS
Leveraging Congregational Infrastructures for Maximum Impact on Disease and Poverty

Andreas Hipple and Jean Duff[1]

As the 2015 deadline for the Millennium Development Goals (MDGs) approaches, and as the likelihood of success appears to be fading, it is useful to recall that the urgency to achieve the goals is not a mere statistical exercise; it is a moral call to save lives and end poverty. With some 29,000 preventable child deaths each day (UNICEF Child Mortality), 77 million children denied access to education (UNICEF News Note: "On Global Action Week on Education, millions of children still not in school"), and 536,000 women dying from the complications of childbirth every year (Women Deliver 2010), the challenge is real and profound. Progress has been made—Egypt, Honduras, Malaysia, and Thailand halved their maternal mortality rates over the past several decades—but this progress is tempered by poor trends in numerous other countries.

To achieve the MDGs requires the creative use of both new and existing resources. National governments and multilateral institutions must seek new public–private partnerships, the full mobilization of civil society, and new ways of working with groups and institutions that can effect sustainable change on a large scale and across the full range of development challenges. When both fully mobilized and resourced, faith institutions—congregations and faith-based organizations—are uniquely placed to help deliver progress on many of the toughest problems.

---

[1]The authors thank Laiah Idelson for impeccable research assistance, and Azza Karam and Matt Weiner for helpful comments on an earlier draft.

While we recognize that religious leaders are persuasive and influential in communities worldwide, this article focuses on faith leaders' power to have a positive impact on achieving the MDGs in sub-Saharan Africa. The MDGs will not be achieved without including the religious leaders and FBOs in the effort. Religious leaders can potentially have an extraordinary impact upon key behaviors through their reach, scale, influence, and sustainability. This article reviews various trends and challenges associated with the inclusion of faith leaders in development—paying special attention to an innovative approach with which the authors are involved—and arguing for the benefits of incorporating religious leaders on an interfaith basis in poverty reduction programs. While interfaith action on the MDGs can and—we believe—should include traditional FBOs and related activities, this article is especially concerned with the mobilization of religious leaders themselves, as there is a particular need to increase their direct engagement on MDG-related issues.

Value added by faith leaders

Attitude and behavior changes on a massive scale are important elements of the successful pursuit of each MDG. For instance, attaining Goals 2 (universal primary education) and 3 (promoting gender equality and empowering women) requires men and women to become more supportive of girls' education, while Goal 5 (improving maternal health) requires families to accept that malaria is preventable and treatable, and to take specific actions such as using insecticide-treated bednets and seeking intermittent preventive treatment during pregnancy. Similar examples can be cited for each of the other goals. The problem is that producing lasting behavior change is among the most difficult challenges that development and public health professionals face.

When, why, and how do people change entrenched behavior? The trillions of private-sector dollars spent on marketing each year tell us that inducing targeted behavior change is neither easy nor cheap. Much of that money, of course, is spent on trying to get a particular message to a potential customer. The most effective marketing campaigns come from sources with credibility, regular access to the target audience to reinforce the messages, and sufficient reach to deliver messages to large numbers of potential customers. In public health messaging, many of the same communications principles apply.

In the development arena, there is often no group better-placed to deliver key messages than local religious leaders. Imams, pastors, priests, and other faith leaders arguably have unparalleled reach, scale, and influence in developing countries, with the relative permanence of their institutions at the local level also potentially adding a significant degree of sustainability if the leaders can be prompted to repeat messaging over time. Weak state institutions in many developing countries mean that the capacity of state agents to reach populations from the most distant villages to the central urban areas is frequently limited. Religious leaders are present in many of the places that state structures struggle to reach, and they have influence over the behaviors of their followers. If they can be engaged to deliver targeted messages, they can help fill a gap in public health delivery. Challenges to this approach include the difficulty of training and mobilizing large numbers of religious leaders, ensuring the accuracy and quality of their messages, and monitoring and evaluation of such interventions.

One example of faith leaders' reach shows the impact they can have, both in a positive and a negative way. In 2003, global efforts to eradicate polio through universal childhood vaccination met with resistance in northern Nigeria, where a number of Muslim leaders, including the Supreme Council for Sharia, issued statements claiming the polio vaccine would make people infertile and/or infected with HIV. As a result, many Muslim families refused to vaccinate their children, causing new epidemics to spread throughout both Nigeria and West Africa. However, when the Sultan of Sokoto and the Emir of Kano, Nigeria's two most prominent Muslim leaders, spoke out against such statements and even had their children vaccinated, resistance to the vaccine campaign began to cease (Yahya 2006). This demonstration of the influence of religious leaders on health-related behavior suggests that engaging them to become positive agents of behavior change can prevent potential problems and produce positive change. It follows that harnessing this comparative advantage by equipping community-based faith leaders to deliver key behavior change communication (BCC) messages can be an effective strategy for addressing the development challenge posed by entrenched behaviors. The comparative advantage may be especially great when attempting to change a repetitive pattern (e.g., sleeping under a net each night) rather than a one-time change (e.g., receiving a vaccine) (McKenzie-Mohr 2000), as faith leaders are especially well-placed to reinforce messages over time—a major challenge to most BCC campaigns.

Reach and scale

Religious institutions—congregational networks, Muslim associations, etc.—extend to the most remote and poorest communities, often reaching where government does not. Through clinics and hospitals that they run, religious organizations are often the sole or primary providers of "end-of-the-road care" to those most in need. In sub-Saharan Africa, faith communities provide an estimated 40 percent of health services. This percentage is even greater in rural areas, and in the poorest and most unstable places, including conflict or post-conflict states. State-run health systems tend to be weak at best in many of these environments, but churches and mosques can be found in the most difficult-to-reach locations. Hospitals and clinics run by religious groups are often the only ones available to the continent's most vulnerable populations (Bandy et al. 2008).

Approximately 75 percent of South Sudan's health services are provided by faith-based institutions, as are roughly half of services in the Democratic Republic of Congo and Zimbabwe (Dimmock 2005). Religious leaders and houses of worship are found throughout these countries. In times of war or political crisis, these institutions do not typically disappear; they become lifelines for people under threat, providing physical and spiritual succor to those who most need it. This presence contributes to the credibility and trust that faith leaders enjoy, ensuring the power of the messages they deliver—be it spiritual guidance or more earthly advice about insecticide-treated nets.

Influence

The strength of faith leaders lies largely in their unparalleled credibility and influence in African communities. According to one study, 90 percent of Africans affiliate themselves with either Christianity or Islam alone (The Pew Forum on Religion and Public Life 2010). Furthermore, 75 percent of Africans identify religious leaders as the group they trust most (Ferret 2005). Faith is an essential part of life in most African settings, from the urban evangelical mega-churches of Lagos to the smallest local mosque in a Tanzanian coastal town. Faith informs and guides behavior on countless levels; indeed, the principal purpose of faith leaders is arguably to influence behavior of their followers such that they act according to the dictates of their faiths. Faith leaders have been in the business of behavior change for millennia.

Giving faith leaders the knowledge and tools to use their influence to change health- and development-related behavior is not, then, a complete departure from their normal activities. In addition, couching behavior change communications messages in religious language and beliefs could make them even more effective. The value and effectiveness of faith-based BCC messages follows directly from the credibility and influence that faith leaders already enjoy. We only have to look to the influence—both positive and negative—of faith leaders on attitude and behavior change related to HIV/AIDS to be convinced of their power over key health-related behaviors. For example, research by Edward C. Green (2001) in Senegal suggests that early attempts to fight HIV/AIDS were hampered by religious leaders claiming infected people suffered a "divine curse." After government and UN agencies educated the religious leaders about HIV, many of them changed their tune and proved keen to take action. Today, faith leaders emphasize abstinence but also promote condoms in an effort to limit both the spread of the disease and the stigma. As a result of faith leaders' education and engagement in the overall program against HIV, Senegal emerged as a success story in combating HIV/AIDS. We argue here that a systematic scaled-up approach to mobilizing faith assets can build on this influence to increase the impact and effectiveness of efforts to target major global health challenges.

Sustainability
From an international development perspective, the pursuit of sustainable change is something akin to seeking the Holy Grail. Many strive for it, but we are not truly convinced that we can find it. Engaging faith communities—which are fundamental building blocks of civil society in much of the developing world—allows development professionals to build programs that are as sustainable as possible. As noted above, faith institutions and leaders are relatively permanent parts of most societies;

they are resilient through periods of turmoil and political change, and many show leadership in taking tough stances against injustice, including challenging and speaking out against society's ills. In 2007, Muslim leaders, as part of the Muslim Council of Imams and Preachers of Kenya, encouraged religious leaders to speak out during Friday prayers against female genital cutting. The hope was to emphasize that the Qur'an does not encourage harm to the body. While religious leaders wished to protect the women of their communities, their stance angered many community members, both men and women. The religious leaders remained steadfast in their determinacy to secure good health and equality for their communities, repeating the message and ultimately making a significant contribution to changes in local behavior (IRIN News 2007). This is evidence that the sustainability of health messages thus can be strengthened by working with strong local religious leaders who are relatively permanent fixtures in local society.

Furthermore, many faith leaders generally exhibit a holistic concern for the whole person, family and community, providing services to diverse members of their communities with a focus on those most in need. Regular interaction between faith leaders and community members—be it at the mosque on Fridays or at Sunday church services—allows the former to reinforce the messages they seek to deliver to the latter. As discussed below, prompting them to do so poses one challenge to tapping into the full potential of religious leaders as development actors.

For the United Nations and others interested in sustainable development, this means that faith institutions have unique access to the people who most need to act in order to facilitate progress on the MDGs. However, deploying the ground forces of faith in the battle against disease, injustice, and poverty requires a significant investment of time, energy, and resources to ensure that they are properly equipped and trained for action. Action that is interfaith in nature has the added potential benefit of contributing to social bridge-building and conflict prevention.

The added value of interfaith approaches

Effectively addressing the major health and development challenges framed by the MDGs requires large-scale community-wide interventions that reach people of all faiths. Most communities in sub-Saharan Africa include people from many different denominations and faiths, as well as indigenous religions. This is true in other regions of the developing world, as well, including many Asian countries. Recognizing this religious diversity, Hajiya Bilkisu Yusuf, a journalist and leading member of the Federation of Muslim Women's Associations in Nigeria (FOMWAN), recently quoted Methodist Bishop Sunday Onuoha, executive director of the Nigerian Inter-Faith Action Association (NIFAA), in an article on the importance of combating malaria from an interfaith perspective:

"This mosquito that causes malaria is a Christian mosquito because it goes to the church on Sunday, listens to the sermon and bites worshippers. It is also a Muslim mosquito because it goes to the mosque on Friday, listens to the sermon, bites worshippers and gives them malaria. Since this mosquito does not respect any religion, we need an interfaith approach to eliminate the menace of this interfaith mosquito!" (Yusuf Mini 2009).

To maximize reach and impact, it is important to engage the full range of a community's religious assets. In addition to providing comprehensive delivery systems that complement state structures, the benefits of interfaith collaboration certainly have the potential to extend to increases in common understanding and harmonious living. Development agencies and national governments, however, often shy away from supporting the work of religious institutions because of a reluctance to cross real boundaries between church and state, and a desire to avoid the appearance of favoring one religious entity over another. These barriers to collaboration between state and religious sectors can be addressed by providing a coordinating mechanism that engages all significant religious entities, thus providing a single interlocutor and partner. Structuring this mechanism as an independent non-governmental organization (NGO) rather than as a religious agency can help ensure the bottom-line development focus of this potential collaboration.

Challenges to interfaith action

Despite the potential gains to be had from increased mobilization of interfaith action in support of achieving the MDGs and other development aims, the United Nations and other donors are far from achieving the full mobilization of religious leaders and structures for development purposes.

There are many varied challenges that groups face when trying to fully include the interfaith sector. Two important and related hurdles are the shortage of human and financial resources available to organize the engagement of religious leaders on development challenges. These limitations cause most projects in this area to be small in scale, with weak or undeveloped links to public-sector institutions such as health and planning ministries that typically lead or regulate activities in the specific sector of intervention. Faith groups working to engage congregational leaders directly—as opposed to the major international FBOs such as Catholic Relief Services and World Vision—typically have weak data on their activities, capacities, and impact. These weaknesses are tied to the resource problem, as the lack of data limits both the types of funding that faith groups are able to receive and the types of partnerships they are able to forge. Opportunities to partner with government agencies and secular development agencies are thus relatively few.

In essence, the resource constraint is largely a "chicken-or-the-egg" type of dilemma: without greater investment of resources, religious mobilization will remain of a small scale and project managers will be unable to conduct the kinds of impact evaluations that can convince potential partners to fund expanded activities, but without demonstrations of impact, those resources are generally not forthcoming. Overcoming this dilemma and attracting these resources will require changes in the way religious leaders and institutions interact with major donors, national governments, development NGOS, and other partners.

Faith and the United Nations

A strong case can be made for increasing the role of faith leaders and religious institutions in international development efforts, although the case still needs to be strengthened with "hard" evidence of impact from surveys and independent research. The major funders appear increasingly open to hearing this case; indeed, strong advocates for engagement of faith leaders have emerged in the UN secretariat and elsewhere. A prominent example is presented by the ambitious undertaking of the United Nations Population Fund (UNFPA) to engage faith leaders in the population and health agenda for women and girls and to launch, at a conference of 160 faith-based organizations (FBOs) from forty-five countries in Istanbul in late 2008, a Global Interfaith Network on Population and Development (Karam 2009).

UNFPA's leaders are deeply committed to increasing the mobilization of faith leaders in support of the MDGs. "Given these quantitative and qualitative realities and the critical personal and community-based connection between the people and the faith-based organization centers providing services, we realized that to become strategic and sustainable, we needed to engage these critical service providers," Thoraya Ahmed Obaid, UNFPA's executive director, noted at a policy roundtable in New York on August 3, 2009. Similar observations have been expressed in other multilateral and international agencies.

Other UN agencies are also getting in on the action. In March 2010, UNAIDS co-hosted a summit in the Netherlands on Religious Leadership in Response to HIV. UNAIDS aimed to encourage religious leaders to generate more positive and sustainable dialogue around ending HIV and its stigma. The conference agenda recognized the full gamut of religious leaders' reach: from the smallest villages to the most influential politicians' offices. Using the pulpit, religious leaders can change their communities' behaviors to prevent the disease, as well as discourage prejudice toward infected people (UNAIDS 2010).

Other bilateral and multilateral donor agencies are encouraging faith-based organizations working on development issues, and provide support for programs, research and advocacy in this area. The U.S. President's Malaria Initiative (PMI) financed a ground-breaking interfaith program against malaria in Mozambique (Duff 2007), and the World Bank's Development Dialogue on Values and Ethics unit supports and conducts significant research into the intersection of faith and development.

National mobilization of the religious sector in partnership with public sector
One new approach to organizing and promoting interfaith action on development issues is emerging from the Center for Interfaith Action on Global Poverty (CIFA) in Washington, DC. CIFA seeks to improve the capacity and effectiveness of the faith community in its collective effort to reduce global poverty and disease. CIFA does this through increased interfaith coordination, best practices and model sharing, innovative

mobilization of resources, and advocacy on behalf of interfaith approaches to development. The CIFA approach complements the work of other important interfaith organizations that generally focus on interfaith dialogue and conflict resolution. For example, Religions for Peace (RFP) has a long track record of organizing inter-religious councils worldwide that provide significant leadership on conflict transformation and advocacy. A number of other interfaith organizations are tackling specific diseases and challenges; for example, the Malawian Interfaith AIDS Association (MIAA) has contributed to Malawi's battle against HIV/AIDS. CIFA differs from RFP in that rather than providing a structure and venue for interfaith dialogue, it seeks to promote a complementary structure for joint action across religious lines; this action can help build trust and thereby indirectly support the interfaith work of RFP and its affiliates. Unlike many single-issue interfaith NGOs, CIFA seeks to help create structures that, while maintaining their independence, are closely tied to state structures as a partner on a variety of health and poverty issues, providing a resource that can strengthen public health systems and systems planning.

CIFA's approach is to establish "Interfaith Action Associations" (IFAAs)—interfaith NGOs based in developing countries that can serve as new coordinating mechanisms to support interfaith public–private partnerships across a variety of development issues. CIFA is able to do this work successfully because it acts as a neutral convener for multiple faith groups to join together on common issues of concern, and because it seeks to build IFAAs as indigenously controlled and managed organizations that are explicitly not subordinate to CIFA. By bringing expertise in development programming and NGO management, CIFA helps national religious leaders create new structures for interfaith collaboration that can tap into existing religious networks and relationships to mobilize faith leaders. These new large-scale interreligious collaborations facilitate the mobilization of religious resources at national levels, can be scaled up or down to address national or local development issues, and are flexible enough to be replicable across diverse national contexts.

Interfaith Action Associations are intended to organize collaborations based on the way that a country's religious leaders are already organized. Rather than re-inventing the wheel, they are designed to collaborate with existing religious organizations that already work with religious leaders. For example, the NIFAA is closely aligned with the Christian Association of Nigeria (CAN) and the Nigerian Supreme Council of Islamic Affairs (NSCIA). In addition, IFAAs provide a voice for a country's faith sector as a whole vis-à-vis pressing development challenges. They are designed to present the sector's unique capacities and activities to global, national, and local stakeholders, both public and private. The IFAA model also provides an organizational structure that can help improve the quality and availability of data relating to faith-based activities in health and poverty reduction. By organizing evidence and making the case for the faith sector as an effective, credible development partner under an interfaith umbrella, IFAAs can be focal points for global advocacy and outreach to increase the share of public and private resources that flow through faith institutions.

The case for increasing such resource flows depends upon an IFAA's capacity to mobilize inter-religious collaboration on poverty issues by leveraging congregational infrastructure (churches, mosques, etc.) for concerted action. This is best illustrated by the case of the NIFAA.

Case study: The Nigerian Model: NIFAA
At the encouragement of the World Bank's Malaria Booster Control Program and the Office of the UN Special Envoy for Malaria, CIFA representatives in early 2009 consulted with the Sultan of Sokoto, leader of the NSCIA, and Archbishop John Onaiyekan, the leader of CAN, to gauge their interest in and support for a new interfaith organization focused on development action, starting with the malaria issue. Both leaders—now co-chairs of NIFAA—indicated strong support for the initiative. By World Malaria Day, April 25, 2009, they joined Nigeria's federal health minister, Professor Babatunde Osotimehin, the UN Special Envoy for Malaria, Ray Chambers, CIFA founder Ed Scott, and other supporters in Washington, DC to announce the launch of NIFAA. The Nigerian Ministry of Health, with World Bank support, committed more than $2 million over two years to fund NIFAA's secretariat in Abuja.

A year later, NIFAA is an active partner of the Nigerian National Malaria Control Programme (NMCP), actively training Muslim and Christian leaders to deliver key malaria messages in conjunction with religious services on Fridays and Sundays. Indeed, the NMCP has included NIFAA as a key partner in its 2010 operational plan. CIFA continues to provide technical assistance to NIFAA from the former's base in Washington, aided by occasional trips to Nigeria, but NIFAA has rapidly established itself as a strong independent organization with a proven capacity to train religious leaders to deliver health messages. It succeeds in mobilizing faith leaders thanks to its close ties to the respective umbrella organizations for Nigeria's two major faith traditions. To strengthen its case for greater program funding, NIFAA is working with the World Bank and other supporters to design survey instruments that provide data on NIFAA's real value added. NIFAA's initial success has attracted the attention of President Obama, who made reference to it in his Accra speech on July 11, 2009, and ex-UK Prime Minister Tony Blair, who visited an NIFAA-organized training outside Abuja in February 2010.

Other budding efforts to invest in interfaith and faith-based approaches
A macro approach to mobilizing faith-based resources is presented by the Women, Faith, and Development Alliance (WFDA), an advocacy campaign that seeks to secure commitments by faith, development, and women's organizations to invest in women's and girls' empowerment. Hundreds of organizations have joined in common cause to reduce poverty through investing in women and girls. After WFDA's global Breakthrough summit in April 2008, regional and national WFDA efforts have been formed, beginning with WFDA Liberia. The WFDA Asia-Pacific Breakthrough in December 2009 saw women's organizations, faith communities and development agencies gather in Melbourne, Australia to launch the Asia-Pacific Women, Faith and Development Alliance to catalyze investment in women and girls within the region. Over $1 billion was raised (Sloan 2010).

Other international organizations are likewise seeking ways to collaborate with faith leaders on an interfaith basis to pursue their development agendas. The Global Fund to Fight AIDS, Tuberculosis, or Malaria (GF) is beginning to allocate resources to faith institutions. In Ethiopia, the Ethiopian Inter-Faith Forum for Development, Dialogue and Action (EIFDDA) was chosen as a Principal Recipient (PR) of a GF grant to address HIV/AIDS. According to its GF proposal, EIFDDA represents 52,600 churches and 125,000 mosques and religious schools (The Global Fund 2007: 32).

The Ethiopian example aside, there have been only eleven different FBOs that have acted as Global Fund PRs since the Fund's creation, out of hundreds of government agencies and NGOs that have been PRs. In the last analysis of 2006 funding, nine FBOs were selected as PRs, along with 488 FBO Sub-Recipients, together accounting for only 5.4 percent of GF resources (The Global Fund 2007).

When it comes to representation at the decision-making and funding tables, the faith sector is at a disadvantage: while 78 percent of the Global Fund's Country Coordinating Mechanisms (CCM) have one faith representative, only 6 percent of CCM representatives worldwide represent the religious sector. Tanzania may be the only country to have the representatives of both Christian and Muslim communities in the CCM. Single-member representation often results in the failure to include the assets and perspectives of diverse national faith communities (Johnson 2008). In addition, these efforts, while faith-based, focus less on mobilizing faith leaders themselves, and more on having faith-inspired organizations implement specific projects.

Conclusion

Increasing the resources allocated to faith institutions is not simply a question of advocating for changes in the way funders do business; faith institutions themselves must increase their visibility and make themselves part of the system that can finance them. Strengthening the evidence base for the capacity, impact and added value of this approach is essential to making the case for funding and scaling up interfaith action. Many of the resources that FBOs provide are unknown to the outside world or seen as a normal part of existing heath service structures. Increased mapping of the services they provide will increase their visibility to government partners, donor agencies, and their own communities. This will give them voice in national, regional, and local government agency planning and funding negotiations. A joint World Health Organization and CIFA consultation in Geneva in November 2009 established an agenda for standard-setting and international collaboration in this regard.

New national-scale partnerships such as that between NIFAA and Nigeria's Federal Ministry of Health offer exciting new possibilities for sustainable impact on MDGs, and, in the long term, lay the groundwork for new partnerships between the religious and public sectors.

The promise of interfaith action has not only captured the imagination of development practitioners around the world; political leaders are likewise coming to see the need to support interfaith action. President Barack Obama, in his Cairo speech on June 4, 2009, remarked that "Around the world, we can turn dialogue into interfaith service, so bridges between peoples lead to action—whether it is combating malaria in Africa, or providing relief after a natural disaster." As resources begin to flow into such interfaith service, there is reason to be hopeful in the struggle to attain the MDGs and make significant progress on other development issues.

Holy texts from almost every faith suggest that if one saves a life, it is as though one has saved all of humanity. Religious leaders and faith-based organizations heed this message and are increasingly ready to engage in the effort to eradicate global poverty and disease; development professionals will do well to seek opportunities to tap into religious networks and equip faith leaders to be foot soldiers in the collective struggle to achieve the MDGs.

Works cited

Bandy, G., Crouch, A., Haenni, C., Holley, P., Larsen, C., Penlington, S., Price, N., Wilkins, C., 2008, in Karpf, T. and Ross, A., eds, *Building from Common Foundations: The World Health Organization and Faith-Based Organizations*, Geneva: World Health Organization, pp. 5–40.

Dimmock, F.E., 2005, "Christian Health Associations in Africa." Paper presented at the 2005 Christian Connections for International Health Annual Conference; 28-31 May 2005; Germantown, MD.

Duff, Jean, 2007, "Together Against Malaria: Faith-Led Community Mobilization in Mozambique," in Marshall, K. and Van Saanen, M., eds., *Development and Faith: Where Mind, Heart, and Soul Work Together*, Washington, DC: The World Bank, pp. 67–75.

Ferret, Grant, 2005, "Africans Trust Religious Leaders," BBC News, Available at: http://news.bbc.co.uk/2/hi/africa/4246754.stm [accessed 2 April 2010].

Green, Edward C., 2001, The Impact of Religious Organizations in Promoting HIV/AIDS Prevention. Presented at "Challenges for the Church: AIDS, Malaria & TB," Christian Connections for International Health, Arlington, VA.

IRIN News, 2007, "Kenya: Religious Leaders Join Anti-FGM Fight." Available at: http://www.irinnews.org/PrintReport.aspx?ReportId=71087# [accessed 13 March 2010].

Johnson, B.A., 2008, *The Global Fund and FBOs: Improving Collaboration and Access to Resources to Fight HIV/AIDS*. Geneva: The Global Fund.

Karam, Azza, 2009, Project Description Prepared for UN ECOSOC Innovation Fair. UNFPA. Available at: http://esango.un.org/innovationfair/notes/unfpa.pdf [accessed 2 April 2010].

McKenzie-Mohr, Doug, 2000, "Promoting Sustainable Behavior: An Introduction to Community-Based Social Marketing," *Journal of Social Issues* 56(3), pp. 543–554. Available at: http://www.rug.nl/psy/onderwijs/firststep/content/papers/2.3.pdf [accessed 28 January 2010].

Sloan, Jane, 2010, "Breaking Through." Available at: http://www.iwda.org.au/au/2009/12/07/breaking-through-jane-sloane/ [accessed 20 February 2010].

The Global Fund, 2007, The Global Fund Annual Report 2007. Geneva: The Global Fund.

The Pew Forum on Religion and Public Life, 2010, "Tolerance and Tension: Islam and Christianity in Sub-Saharan Africa." Available at: http://pewforum.org/docs/?DocID=516 [accessed 26 April 2010].

UNAIDS, 2010, "Religious Summit Engages Religious Leaders in the HIV Response." Available at: http://www.aegis.org/news/unaids/2010/UN100328.html [accessed 13 March 2010].

Women Deliver, 2010, "Maternal Health." Available at: http://www.womendeliver.org/knowledge-center/facts-figures/maternal-health/?facts/maternal.htm [accessed 2 April 2010].

Yahya, Maryam, 2006, *Polio Vaccines – Difficult to Swallow: The Story of a Controversy in Northern Nigeria*. Brighton: Institute of Development Studies.

Yusuf Mini, Bilkisu, 2009, "The Interfaith Mosquito," Leadership Nigeria. Available at: http://www.leadershipnigeria.com/index.php/columns/views/features/10034-that-interfaith-mosquito [accessed 14 January 2010].

CROSSCURRENTS

THE UN SYSTEM AND RELIGIOUS ACTORS IN THE CONTEXT OF GLOBAL CHANGE

Josef Boehle

Introduction

Past political efforts of achieving large-scale global systemic change have been successful if they have been rooted in and supported by large alliances of non-governmental and civil society organizations. The examples of the movements for banning land mines and for the establishment of an International Criminal Court, the *Jubilee 2000* campaign and the *Make Poverty History* campaign are some of the more recent examples. The fall of the Berlin Wall in Germany caused by a grassroots citizen movement, supported by Christian communities in the former East Germany, as well as the Solidarnosc trade union movement supported by the Catholic Church in Poland, are among the best known examples of recent history where citizen movements and religious actors joint forces.

Given that the pre-eminent global forum, where regular interactions of NGOs, transnational civil society networks and governments take place is the UN System and given the importance of citizen movements and religious actors for sustainable global change, a closer look at how civil society and religious actors engage with the UN System can make an important contribution both to analysis and strategic planning when responding to contemporary global challenges.

In this article, I will look at religious actors in the wider context of global civil society and in the context of the UN System, then look at the pioneering programs for engaging with religious actors that have been developed within UNESCO, and finally reflect on the crucial contribution that religious actors are making to development cooperation and the achievement of the Millennium Development Goals (MDGs).

Alliances between grassroots movements, non-profit organizations, religious communities, and spiritual organizations, supported by religious and spiritual leaders, can have an immense global impact. The *Jubilee 2000* debt relief campaign for poor countries is one example of such an alliance across a great diversity of participating groups that had won the support of many religious leaders and communities. Other less well-known examples of the influence of global movements of religious NGOs are, for example, the participation of religious and spiritual organizations in the UNESCO led Global Movement for a Culture of Peace and the support of religious and spiritual organizations for the 2001-2010 *UN Decade for a Culture of Peace and Non-violence for the Children of the World* (Boehle, 2001, p. 217–218). NGOs often start the initial initiatives that result years later in changes in national and international law, in (re)forming international values and norms, and in (re)shaping international institutions and their programs. For example, seen from a long-term perspective, it can be argued that it was the over 100-years-old international interreligious movement with its countless events and activities throughout the last century that prepared the ground for the major international interreligious events during the last decade like the *Millennium World Peace Summit* held in New York in 2000 or the "High-level Dialogue on Interreligious and Intercultural Understanding and Cooperation for Peace" of the UN General Assembly in 2007 (http://www.un.org/ga/president/62/issues/hld-interreligious.shtml).

The *"Millennium World Peace Summit"* (28–31 August 2000) brought together more than 1,000 senior religious, spiritual, and indigenous leaders from over 50 countries at the UN to address together major world problems and increase interreligious understanding and cooperation (Boehle, Josef 2001, p. 230ff). In *Development and Faith*, a book of case studies from around the world of religious organizations engaging with development and peace issues, Marshall and van Saanen point to the Millennium World Peace Summit and its impact:

Yet since that meeting in 2000, faith groups have steadily intensified their engagement in the MDG framework, and religious actors are now poised to play even more significant roles. The major areas of engagement include national, regional, and global advocacy and mobilization around the MDGs; implementing specific programs to help fulfill them; and monitoring progress. (Marshall and van Saanen, 2007, p. 24)

More recently, a major global event was the *"High-level Dialogue on Interreligious and Intercultural Understanding and Cooperation for Peace"* (4, 5, and 8 October 2007), the first formal high-level session of the UN General Assembly to address issues of interreligious and intercultural understanding and cooperation and included an interactive hearing with civil society.

If we apply the same model of change (citizen movements, NGOs, and religious actors as crucial participants in sustainable global change processes) to the challenges faced by the international community to achieve the UN *Millennium Development Goals*, one can conclude that as important as high-level meetings and summits at the United Nations and as important as the work of various UN agencies, and next to the support from governmental development agencies, a popular, global NGO movement, including religious NGOs and religious communities, can make a crucial difference for the achievement of the MDGs. Such a scenario would also suggest that the contributions of RNGOs are not only important for service delivery and humanitarian assistance at country level, but also for advocacy and policy development internationally. Thomas (2005) supports a similar analysis when he states:

> The global religious subcultures and the new religious movements facilitated by globalization are as much a part of world politics as the secular NGOs that are a part of global civil society. These religious actors will also play an important role in shaping the contours of world politics in the twenty-first century, and need to become a part of the study of international relations. (Thomas, 2005, p. 98)

Religious NGOs/FBOs as part of transnational civil society at the United Nations

The emergence of a global civil society is one of the most significant historic developments after the end of the Cold War. Many believe that we are living today in an increasingly tri-polar world, determined by three main forces: governments, business, and the global civil society. Nicanor Perlas writes in his book *Shaping Globalization: Civil Society, Cultural Power and Threefolding*:

> We now live in a tri-polar world where the forces, capacities, and resources to change the world are clustered in the hands of business, governments, and the global civil society. In many countries and towns, another constellation of forces is becoming increasingly visible. Three global powers are now determining the understanding and fate of burning global issues. (Perlas, 2000, p. 1)

Partnerships emerge across the boundaries of governments, business, and global civil society. David Cooperrider and other leading scholars in organizational research analyzed the rising potential for global cooperation in *Organizational Dimensions of Global Change. No Limits to Cooperation*, a book addressing the changes in our global age from a perspective of organizational theory and development. He wrote:

> The first is to underscore the point that it really is no longer utopian or romantically idealistic to be using the language of global change. The development of global co-operative capacity, across boundaries of all kinds, is part of the evolution of human efforts to organize life in response to transboundary problems and opportunities. We believe that these processes will accelerate in coming years. The second is to bring attention to what we feel is a vast opportunity for organisation theory. Indeed, the observable fact is this: Since World War II, more than 30.000 transnational nongovernmental (NGO) and intergovernmental (IGO) organizations have emerged to manage concerns related to issues of ecology and development (Union of International Associations, 1997). (Cooperrider, 1999, p. 11)

We see increasingly the emergence of transnational civil society networks working on the critical issues of our time, including on issues of poverty and development. The increase in networking among RNGOs, religious communities and inter-religious organizations is closely related to these wider developments in the field of civil society organizations and movements.

Ann M. Florini in *The Third Force: The Rise of Transnational Civil Society* wrote about today's transnational civil society and the impact of these organizations, alliances and networks. She prefers to use the term "transnational civil society" instead of "global civil society" as she finds that most movements and networks are not really global, but have a greater strength in some regions of the world:

> We use the somewhat ungainly term "transnational civil society "in preference to other frequently heard lingo (such as "global civil society") to emphasize both the border-crossing nature of the links and the fact that rarely are these ties truly global, in the sense of involving groups and individuals from every part of the world. The Middle East and sub-Saharan Africa in particular are severely underrepresented in transnational nongovernmental coalitions, other than those that address strictly regional and developmental concerns. (Florini, 2000, p. 7)

Transnational civil society organizations are coming together around shared values and address specific issues, like the "International Campaign to Ban Landmines" (Florini, 2000, p. 6, 7). Civil society emerges as the third force, next to business and governments. Next to the discussion and evaluation on what place and influence civil society has on national levels, it is now time, according to Ann M. Florini, to assess the role of transnational civil society in an age of globalization: "[A]s globalization proceeds, it will stimulate more transnational civil society formation. And that, in turn, will influence how globalization proceeds. So far, the debate on the role of transnational civil society has been confined largely to polemical broadsides and scholarly journals. It is now time for a broader debate" (Florini, p. 12).

The pre-eminent global forum, where regular interactions of NGOs, transnational civil society networks, and governments take place, is the

UN System. In this forum, religious NGOs are very active and they have engaged with the UN ever since its foundation. They are a part of United Nations–civil society relations as defined by UN Charter article 71: "The Economic and Social Council may make suitable arrangements for consultation with non-governmental organizations which are concerned with matters within its competence. Such arrangements may be made with international organizations and, where appropriate, with national organizations after consultation with the Member of the United Nations concerned" (UN Charter, Chapter X, Article 71).

The engagement of secular and faith-based NGOs/FBOs with the UN has continued to grow over the years and there are now over 4,000 NGOs affiliated with the UN. The precise number is difficult to state as some NGOs (668 NGOs; October 2009) are affiliated with both, the Department for Public Information (DPI) (1664 affiliated NGOs; October 2009) and the Economic and Social Council (ECOSOC) (3052 affiliated NGOs; October 2009); in addition, some NGOs are only accredited with the Commission on Sustainable Development (Boehle, 2007, p. 21). Among the over 4,000 UN accredited NGOs there are 263 religious NGOs accredited through ECOSOC or DPI according to a study by Julia Berger (Berger, 2003, p. 21).

A good example, to illustrate the role which RNGOs frequently play at the UN, is the major contribution made by RNGOs in organizing the *Millennium Forum* of NGOs at the United Nations, 22–26 May 2000 (over 1,000 NGOs and civil society groups participated).

Techeste Ahderom, principal representative to the United Nations for the *Bahá'í International Community*, was cochair of the *Millennium Forum*. Kathleen L. Uhler, OSF, codirector of Franciscans International, was the Executive Secretary of the Millennium Forum. The offices of the Baha'i International Community and of the Franciscans International in New York have been the backbone for the administration of the *Millennium Forum*. The *Millennium Forum* at the UN was one of the most prominent examples of the emerging global civil society and its efforts to find an organizational home in the context of the UN System. The *Millennium Forum* also contributed significantly to the debate that helped to shape the MDGs. These efforts had the full support of former UN Secretary-General Kofi Annan who opened the *Millennium Forum* in the General Assembly Hall and who welcomed often in his speeches the contribution of civil society (Boehle, Josef 2001, pp. 222, 223).

The high attendance at the *Millennium Forum* was a clear sign of a widespread consensus among NGOs and other civil society organizations that a strengthened and more open United Nations is needed. The outcomes of the *Millennium Forum*, however, have been limited by the fact that global civil society struggles itself to get better organized and to come to commonly held positions. In the midst of the many presentations and working groups at the *Millennium Forum*, the question was often asked how to get better organized in future. One outcome of the *Millennium Forum* was the *We the Peoples Millennium Forum Declaration and Agenda for Action: strengthening the United Nations for the twenty-first century* (UN doc. A/54/959) that was distributed to all Heads of States attending the Millennium Summit at the United Nations in September 2000 (Boehle, Josef 2001, p. 223).

Before the *Millennium Forum* took place, Kofi Annan had frequently invited NGOs and civil society organizations to take an active part in shaping and renewing the United Nations. For example, in Wellington, New Zealand, at Victoria University, Annan gave an address to representatives of the United Nations Association of New Zealand, the New Zealand Institute for International Affairs and other non-governmental organizations. There, on the 23 February 2000, Annan spoke of the accomplishments between the United Nations and civil society and the ways in which ties could be strengthened in the future:

> As we begin the twenty-first century, both civil society and the United Nations can look back on some impressive accomplishments. But better still, we can look ahead to what we might accomplish together in the future. Looking ahead, I see a world of opportunities for stronger ties between us. I see a United Nations keenly aware that if the global agenda is to be properly addressed, a partnership with civil society is not an option; it is a necessity. I see a United Nations which recognizes that the NGO revolution—the new global people-power—is the best thing that has happened to our Organization in a long time. (UN Press Release SG/SM/7318, *Partnership With Civil Society Necessity In Addressing Global Agenda*, UN, 2000)

One of the most difficult aspects of a transformation of the United Nations System would be to change the organization from a heavily government-orientated global institution toward a much more open and inclusive institution. In this respect, any required changes to the legal framework of the United Nations or, even more so, any amendments to the UN Charter, would clearly pose immense challenges to the established status quo, challenges which seem almost impossible to solve given the strong self-interests of nation states. A further formalized and legalized participation of civil society at the UN would also make a contribution to a concept of "global governance" that sees global governance as the responsibility of many diverse constituencies. A global governance that, while being led by nation states, would also be open to many other constituencies.

The Millennium momentum, at the end of the 1990s and the beginning of the 21st century, had offered the possibility to bring these then widely debated issues from the discussion in informal settings onto the political agenda of the United Nations.

In the Report "We, the People," submitted by Kofi Annan to the UN General Assembly in March 2000 and presented to the Millennium Summit of Heads of States in September 2000, the importance of a wider participation in global governance was recognized and encouraged:

> Better governance means greater participation, coupled with accountability. Therefore, the international public domain—including the United Nations—must be opened up further to the participation of the many actors whose contributions are essential to managing the path of globalization. Depending on the issues at hand, this may include civil society organizations, the private sector, parliamentarians, local authorities, scientific associations, educational institutions and many others. (Annan, 2000, Report of the UN Secretary-General, We, the Peoples, paragraph 46, p. 8)

In the late 1990s, after the demise of the Cold War and before the rise of the global threat of terrorism, new ideas on how to address major global challenges were debated frequently in many international fora, probably with more optimism then today.

In the year 1997, John W. Holmes Memorial Lecture on *The Imperative of Idealism* was hosted by the Academic Council on the United Nations System (ACUNS); James S. Sutterlin, a former Director of the Executive Office of the UN Secretary-General, came to a conclusion that is increasingly held by many scholars and NGO activists:

> This leads me to a conclusion that I long rejected as unrealistic: civil society must be given a participatory role in the United Nations and one large enough to give the people a sense of responsibility for the organization. As is well-known, this is not a new idea. I would add only the insistence that to bring about a new image of the UN as representative of peoples' as well as governments' interests, civil society must be involved in some way in the decision-making process, perhaps in the form of a second advisory chamber of the General Assembly, where the focus would be on the liberal agenda of the UN system rather than on the machinery for its implementation. . . . The myth of a world community of a thousand cultures joined in freedom and a common oneness with the world they share must become a determining subliminal guide for governments and people toward a new stage of human development. (Sutterlin, 1997, p. 17–18)

Sutterlin concluded in his lecture that a stronger participation of civil society in the United Nations is essential for a renewal of the organization. By giving prominence to civil society organizations he is giving prominence, conceptually speaking, to what in political science is often referred to as "soft power," the power to attract others to your own position, using the means of culture, values, and ideas. The concept of soft power was popularized by Joseph Nye in the 1990s (Nye 1990, 2004).

The brief reflection in this article on global civil society and global governance also highlights the specific role that religious communities and religious NGOs are playing. An argument frequently expressed by prominent religious leaders, RNGO leaders, scholars as well as politicians, is that the unique ethical, material and spiritual resources of the world's religious communities can make a major contribution to tackling the critical issues of our time (climate change, peacebuilding, poverty, terrorism, pandemics, etc.), especially through collaborative efforts in multi-stakeholder coalitions (Boehle, Josef 2001, 2002, 2007). Among the early voices of prominent politicians seeking constructive engagement with religious actors was, for example, Richard von Weizsäcker, a former President of Germany. In a contribution to Hans Küng's book *Yes to a Global Ethic* (1996), von Weizsäcker reflected on the common challenges that the both, the United Nations and the world's religions, need to address in today's world of increasingly global problems. He concluded that religions have to give up living in conflict with each other and instead mobilize their ethical potential for a more peaceful and humane society:

> One of the central tasks of a reform of the United Nations at the beginning of its second half-century will be not merely just to continue to counter the symptoms of the dangers to security with weapons, but to identify their causes with other than military means and to help to eradicate them, especially in the sphere of social and economic tasks, human rights and development. . . . Credibility is the issue. It can only be grounded in collaboration, in ecumenical reflection. The task of the religions is not to lure the faithful in the name of their own doctrines and rules, but to make a contribution to the pacification and humanization of our society. (Weizsäcker, in: Küng, 1996, p. 30–32)

"Religions and the UN" is a subject that has attracted more and more attention over the last years. On 18 June 2004 the Archbishop of Canterbury, Dr. Rowan Williams, gave a major speech commenting on international relations, the United Nations and the search for a global order which would be more able to respond to today's global challenges. In his speech on *Internationalism and Beyond* he said:

> To summarise, then: the role of the UN remains indispensable, but if it is to function as it needs to in our present context it will need the sort of reshaping tentatively begun and outlined already in the plans that have been advanced in the last couple of years. The Security Council has to recover credibility and enlarge the scope of representation. But the main point that recurs in discussion of the future of international affairs and transnational justice is that

the UN will need to incorporate more clearly the voice of NGOs, of "global civil society," because, in the globalised economy and the globalised information network, the mere brokerage of the interests of individual states is unlikely to deliver long term security . . . Only a morally robust UN can, realistically, draw up and help to realise the elements of a democratic compact. For this, the contribution of religious communities will be essential—though it is also a challenge to those communities to develop with appropriate rigour a theology of democratic accountability and environmental care. (Williams, 2004)

Within the UN System there have been an increasing number of efforts over the past two decades to engage more strategically and in a sustained way with the world of religions. UNESCO was, probably, the first UN agency to develop ongoing programs to reach out to religious actors.

UNESCO addressing intercultural and interreligious issues[1]

Since the early 1990s, UNESCO played a pioneering role in seeking to understand and engage with religious and spiritual communities. Other UN system organizations and programs have also worked with diverse faith communities (UNEP, UNFPA, UNICEF, Alliance of Civilizations, World Bank, etc.), but UNESCO is the leading UN agency on these issues, in terms of both its mandate and its programs.

In recognition of the increasing threat of conflicts between religions and the extensive debate on the role of civilizations in the context of globalization, UNESCO has given attention to the role of religions and cultures in peace-building to prevent conflicts and to foster peace and cooperation across civilizations, cultures and religions. A summary of the beginning of the developments within UNESCO recognizing the role of religions in a Culture of Peace is given in the Final Report of the *UNESCO Conference on the Contribution by Religions to the Culture of Peace* that took place in Barcelona, Spain from the 12–18 December 1994 (Centre UNESCO de Catalunya 1995).

Since 1993, UNESCO has held many conferences addressing the question of religion in conflict situations and in creating a culture of peace. At the 1994 UNESCO conference in Barcelona (December 12–18), a groundbreaking document, *The Declaration on the Role of Religion in the Promotion of a Culture of Peace*, was issued. This remarkable declaration speaks of the major challenges that the world community faces at the turn of the millennium and addresses the core issues of peace, justice, and sustainability. It focuses on the core concerns of the international interreligious movement: working for peace, preventing conflict, reducing poverty, fostering social justice, providing adequate education, respecting the earth and all living beings, and promoting dialogue and harmony among religions (Centre UNESCO de Catalunya 1994). In 1998, UNESCO issued a *Report on Follow up to and Dissemination of the Barcelona Declaration on the Role of Religion in the Promotion of a Culture of Peace*, which attempted to give an assessment of the declaration's impact. The declaration had found widespread recognition and support, many international organizations endorsed it, and further meetings on similar subjects were stimulated. The report noted that by 1998 a total of 13,408 individuals and 309 institutions had endorsed the declaration (UNESCO 1998: 35).

Within UNESCO's culture sector there is a *Division for Cultural Policies and Intercultural Dialogue* and it is here that a program on *Spiritual Convergence and Intercultural Dialogue* started the *Roads of Faiths* project in 1992. International interreligious conferences were held and, for example, the UNESCO conference in Rabat, Morocco (1995) focused on the three monotheistic religions of Judaism, Christianity and Islam, whereas the conference in Valetta, Malta (1997) moved toward addressing interreligious dialogue and understanding in a more pluralistic context. Since then, the Intercultural Dialogue Division and its Interreligious Dialogue Program in the culture sector of UNESCO have continued to co-organize symposia and conferences addressing interreligious themes, often with a regional focus.

Recent UNESCO cosponsored conferences in this series included, for example, a conference in Melbourne (2005) addressing the issue of *Religion in Peace and Conflict: Responding to Fundamentalism and Militancy* and a conference in Moscow (2007) on *Intercultural and Interreligious Dialogue for Peace and Sustainable Development* (organized within the framework of the UNESCO flagship activity *"Promotion of Interfaith Dialogue"*).

Another important part of UNESCO's strategy concerning interreligious issues is the development and further expansion of its network of UNESCO chairs with expertize in related academic subjects. These

UNESCO chairs, based at many universities, can provide expertize on specific issues, religions and regions of the world and are linked in a network. UNESCO's Network on *Inter-religious Dialogue for Intercultural Understanding* currently includes 23 chairs.

The UNESCO report on the "Promotion of religious and cultural understanding, harmony and cooperation," submitted to the UN General Assembly in August 2004 by UNESCO's Director-General Koichi Matsuura, provided an overview on related UNESCO activities and includes policy recommendations. It stresses "the need for education to respect and reflect cultural diversity and to contribute to intercultural understanding and cooperation" (Matsuura, 2004, p.5). In its conclusions and recommendations, the report also calls for the strengthening of the UNESCO Chairs concerned with intercultural and interreligious dialogue (Matsuura, 2004, p. 12).

The above examples of some of UNESCO's work for peace-building and interreligious understanding are only one part of the many international efforts that are being made all around the globe to change the culture of war and violence in which we presently live.

As a global institution, UNESCO has played a pioneering role in seeking ways to get religious communities and NGOs involved in conflict prevention, dialogues and peace education. Such a constructive and proactive approach is more promising for peace-building than is waiting passively for the next downward spirals of conflicts and wars to happen.

International relations and development cooperation

One area in international relations where multi-stakeholder partnerships involving religious actors could make a very significant contribution to global change is development cooperation. Engaging with religious actors could dramatically improve the chances to achieve the UN *Millennium Development Goals*. Over the past decade, a new focus on "religion and development" has grown internationally and new initiatives and programs have been developed in many parts of the world. The *Global Interfaith Network on Population and Development,* facilitated by UNFPA; the *World Faiths Development Dialogue* now based at the *Berkley Center for Religion, Peace and World Affairs,* Georgetown University, USA and the *Religion and Development Program Consortium* based at the University of Birmingham, UK are just three examples of leading contemporary efforts to re-assess and, where possible, advance development cooperation in engaging with religious actors.

Klein Goldewijk in the book *Religion, International Relations and Development Cooperation* (2007) facilitated as editor a wide-ranging reflection on the many aspects of religion in public life in contemporary global contexts. She applied in this book a wide definition of development cooperation:

> The notion of development cooperation can be understood in the general sense of partnerships in support of poverty eradication, sustainable growth, good governance, democracy, human rights and gender equality, being some of the key elements to improve livelihoods and human security in the international community. (Klein Goldewijk, 2007, p. 24)

Such a wide approach to development cooperation and partnerships can provide a strong argument for the necessity to include all the relevant major constituencies into international development policy debates, including a comprehensive debate of the role of religion. The book conducts this debate, for example, by reflecting on the challenges religion poses to contemporary Western paradigms (e.g., the secularization thesis, the Westphalian state-model) as well as by asking what the genuine, positive contribution of religion could be, seen from a diversity of religious and cultural perspectives. Development cooperation is today one of the critical issues in international relations and religious actors play worldwide a significant, but often underestimated role. International Relations today has a meaning that goes beyond a state-centered focus (Klein Goldewijk, 2007, p. 24). If International Relations is seen from such a wide perspective, including non-state actors, then religious actors need to be included in the analysis of the key forces that shape international relations.

In recent years, the growing literature that tries to understand development issues not only from secular perspectives, but also includes religious and spiritual perspectives when seeking to make progress in reducing poverty, enhancing education or eradicating epidemic diseases, signals the beginning of a sea change, the dissolution of paradigms that have dominated public discourse for much of the past century:

Development discourse and policy in the second half of the twentieth century was largely secular and technocratic in character (although as Linden makes clear in this collection, that secular nature hid strong faith undercurrents). It emphasised the rational at the expense of the spiritual and organised religions were often seen as a significant source of opposition to government and donor policies in critical areas such as HIV/AIDS, gender relations and human rights. (Gerald Clarke and Michael Jennings (eds.), 2008, Introduction p. 4.)

Scientific and political paradigms with strong roots in Western culture, often dominated by a *Westphalian* understanding of statehood and by epistemologies that are grounded in the historical experience of the European Enlightenment, are increasingly being challenged in today's global public discourse. The role of religion and spirituality in the public sphere, in civil society, in development cooperation and in global governance is being re-assessed and reconstructed. Thomas (2005), for example, reflects on the application of the concept of "epistemic communities" to religious communities in the theory of international relations, following an argument made by Hoeber Rudolph and Piscatori (1997). The concept of epistemic communities, he summarizes,

> now has been used by some scholars to theorize about the role of religion in a conception of world politics as a global public square, a densely packed, crosscutting arena of key individuals, states, and non-state actors that form various types of transnational solidarities and transnational communities as part of a global or transnational civil society. In other words, the solidarity of religious transnationalism is only one of the types of transnational solidarity in world politics. (Thomas, 2005, p. 108)

A critical reflection on religion and development clearly needs to address both sides of religion: the positive potential of religions to inspire, to sustain communities, to enter into long-term commitments, to foster compassion, to seek justice and to empower the poor; but also the dogmatic and sectarian side of religion, which can lead to discrimination, to divisiveness, to resistance to pragmatic solutions because of strongly held ideological positions, to inequality between men and women, between believers and non-believers.

Conclusion

The nations of the world have made over the last 90 years (first through the League of Nations and now through the United Nations) efforts to move toward a world community, efforts with many setbacks, interrupted by World War II and seriously limited by the Cold War period and today's major economic differences.

However, even today the United Nations System is seen as rather helpless in the face of global problems and in most cases the political and economic interests of individual nation states determine the decisions or, sometimes, the absence of decisions. In reality we cannot yet speak of a world community, rather of a crises management system trying to address major world problems, most often with too little power and resources, and often too late. Could a renewed United Nations System, which is more democratic in its structures and significantly expanded to cooperate with and empower NGOs and civil society organizations, religious communities and movements, be more effective in achieving the stated goal of the United Nations to save "succeeding generations from the scourge of war" and in addressing the great challenges of our time? The answer is a clear "yes." No isolated part of the emerging global community can hope to solve today's global problems on its own.

The material infrastructure, and the ethical and spiritual resources of religious and spiritual traditions, are needed to address interconnected and global issues like justice, human rights, peace, and sustainability. Advancing global change through sustainable and large-scale multi-stakeholder partnerships must be accompanied by a substantial change within the UN System. This would create the capacity within the UN System for meaningful institutional cooperation and alliance building with wider parts of the world community. Religious and spiritual individuals all over the world have together begun to reflect and to act on their global responsibilities, so that we can live in a more peaceful, just, and sustainable world community. Now it is time for political institutions, locally, nationally, and internationally, to respond constructively and to further develop the necessary structural frameworks and programs to enable sustainable collaboration with very diverse constituencies, including religious actors. A better future is achievable by human beings united in their respect for diversity.

Works cited

Reports and other documentary publications:

Annan, Kofi, 2000 Report of the UN Secretary-General Kofi Annan to the Millennium Assembly, *We the Peoples*. The Role of the United Nations in the Twenty-first Century, (United Nations Document A/54/2000, 27 March 2000).

Centre UNESCO de Catalunya, 1994 Declaration on the Role of Religion in the Promotion of a Culture of Peace, Barcelona.

Centre UNESCO de Catalunya, 1995 The Contribution by Religions to the Culture of Peace: Final Report, LDB-22224/95, Barcelona.

Matsuura, Koichi, 2004 Report of the Director-General of UNESCO (A/59/201), responding to the General Assembly Resolution (A/RES/58/128) "Promotion of Religious and Cultural Understanding, Harmony and Cooperation."

UN Press Release, Partnership with Civil Society Necessity in Addressing Global Agenda (United Nations Document SG/SM/7318, 2000).

UNESCO, 1998 Report on Follow-up to and Dissemination of the Barcelona Declaration on the Role of Religion in the Promotion for a Culture of Peace, Paris: UNESCO.

We the Peoples Millennium Forum Declaration and Agenda for Action: Strengthening the United Nations for the Twenty-first Century (United Nations Document A/54/959, 8 August 2000).

Web sites:

Millennium Forum Declaration and Agenda for Action. http://www.un.org/millennium/declaration.htm

UN and Civil Society. http://www.un.org/issues/civilsociety/

UN General Assembly, High-level Dialogue on Interreligious and Intercultural Understanding and Cooperation for Peace, 4, 5, and 8 October 2007: http://www.un.org/ga/president/62/issues/hld-interreligious.shtml

UN Millennium Development Goals. http://www.un.org/millenniumgoals/

UN Millennium Development Goals Monitor. http://www.mdgmonitor.org

UN Millennium Summit: http://www.un.org/millennium/

Articles and books:

Berger, Julia, 2003, "Religious Non-Governmental Organisations: An Exploratory Analysis," *VOLUNTAS: International Journal of Voluntary and Nonprofit Organizations* 14 (1), pp. 15–39.

Boehle, Josef, 2001, Inter-religious Co-operation in a Global Age, PhD Thesis, Birmingham: University of Birmingham.

Boehle, Josef, 2002, "Inter-religious Cooperation and Global Change: From a Clash of Civilizations to a Dialogue of Civilizations," *Pacifica Review: Peace, Security and Global Change* 14(3), pp. 227–234.

Boehle, Josef, 2007, "Religions, Civil Society and the UN System," *Studies in Interreligious Dialogue* 17(1), pp. 20–30.

Clarke, Gerard, and Michael Jennings (eds), 2008, *Development, Civil Society and Faith-Based Organisations: Bridging the Sacred and the Secular*, London: Palgrave Macmillan.

Cooperrider, David L., and Jane E. Dutton (eds), 1999, *Organisational Dimensions of Global Change. No Limits to Cooperation*, Thousand Oaks, CA: Sage Publications.

Florini, Ann M., (ed.), 2000, *The Third Force: The Rise of Transnational Civil Society*, Washington and Tokyo: Carnegie Endowment for International Peace, Washington, D.C. and the Japan Center for International Exchange, Tokyo.

Hoeber Rudolph, Susanne, and James Piscatori (eds.), 1997, *Transnational Religion and Fading States*, Boulder, CO: Westview Press.

Klein Goldewijk, Berma (ed.), 2007, *Religion, International Relations and Development Cooperation*, Wageningen: Wageningen Academic Publishers.

Marshall, Katherine, and Marisa van Saanen, 2007, *Development and Faith. Where Mind, Heart and Soul Work Together*, Washington: The World Bank.

Nye, Joseph, 1990, *Bound to Lead: The Changing Nature of American Power*, New York: Basic Books.

Nye, Joseph, 2004, *Soft Power, The Means to Success in World Politics*, Washington DC: Public Affairs.

Perlas, Nicanor, 2000, *Shaping Globalization. Civil Society, Cultural Power and Threefolding*, Quezon City: Center for Alternative Development Initiatives.

Sutterlin, James S., 1997, *The Imperative of Idealism*, ACUNS: John W. Holmes Memorial Lecture.

Thomas, Scott M., 2005, *The Global Resurgence of Religion and the Transformation of International Relations*, New York: Palgrave Macmillan.

Weizsäcker, Richard von, 1996, "Towards a Shared Global Ethic," in Hans Küng, ed., *Yes to a Global Ethic*, London: SCM Press, pp. 29–33.

Williams, Rowan, 2004, "Internationalism and Beyond," Speech given on 18 June 2004, Greenwich, Connecticut. See Archive: http://www.archbishopofcanterbury.org/1204.

Note

1. The following brief account of some of UNESCO's key interreligious activities is a revised and updated version of an earlier summary that was originally published by the author in Religions, Civil Society and the UN System, *Studies in Interreligious Dialogue*, 17 (2007) 1.

CROSSCURRENTS

BRINGING COMMUNITIES CLOSER
The Role of the Alliance of Civilizations (AoC)[1]

Thomas Uthup

How can global divides, particularly in the area of culture, be bridged? One answer has been the Alliance of Civilizations (AoC), established in July 2005 at the initiative of the Governments of Spain and Turkey under the auspices of the United Nations. The Alliance's *raison d'être* is to fill the need to build bridges between societies, promote dialogue and understanding, and forge the collective political will to address the world's imbalances.[2] It aims at doing this through practical actions that will assist in diminishing hostility and promoting harmony among nations and cultures of the world.

These practical projects, outlined in the High Level Group Report, lie in the areas of youth, education, media, and migration because of the conviction that these sectors and actors are critical in creating bridges between cultures, building trust, reconciliation, and mutual respect among diverse communities. These projects exist at the macro-level—such as projects facilitated by the Alliance as well as projects at interregional and national levels—and at the micro-level (or grassroots level) where projects are promoted or highlighted by the Alliance. Thus, in the area of youth, young people are empowered to develop their own cross-cultural projects and promoting exchanges across cultural divides; in the area of media, the conversation about cross-cultural issues is broadened by providing journalists access to a wide range of analysts and commentators; in the area of education, the emphasis is on developing a critical understanding of intercultural issues and providing resources to spread knowledge about diverse religions and beliefs; and in the area of migration, it is about sharing knowledge on innovative integration policies and advancing the debate on managing diversity in multicultural societies.

The Alliance emerged partly out of a concern that polarization between the West (comprising Europe and North America, to a large extent) and the Muslim world (which includes a diversity of communities and cultures including countries such as Albania, Bangladesh, Indonesia, Senegal, and Yemen as well as Muslim minorities in places such as India, Nigeria, the United States, and Europe) was increasing and that there was a need to address this growing divide. There can be no doubt that events such as 9/11, the Madrid bombings, and the Iraq and Afghanistan wars fed into the fears that there was a divide between the so-called Western world and the "Muslim" world. Therefore, the Alliance in dealing with cultural divides must necessarily deal with real—or perceived—religious divides.

When religion as such is seen as one of the parties in the divide, it relates to religion and its impact on the public sphere. Naturally, the Alliance must address religion and religious issues in bridging divides between people. We live in a time when religious communities and faith-based organizations are playing an increasingly significant role in the public sphere. They also retain a wide-ranging influence on the behavior and beliefs of millions of people. Faith-based organizations have major regional and global reach and possess great mobilizing power. Religious leaders play an important part in setting the scene at the local level and shape debates on a number of pressing issues, from social policy to humanitarian relief and the need to address long-standing political conflicts. The influence of religion and religious leaders can be deployed for both good and ill.

The Alliance recognizes that its thinking in this area is constantly evolving, and its work focuses on practical actions rather than methodological and terminological issues. Therefore, in the first part of this essay, I first outline my personal conceptualizations of some key words and concepts that recur in the language of the United Nations relating to religion and one potential model of theoretical thinking about the work of the Alliance. In the second part, I turn to the work of the Alliance of Civilizations and outline its ongoing and emerging activities with religion and faith-based organizations. In the concluding part, I offer some thoughts on the challenges, recommendations, and ideas on dealing with religious groups.

Part I: Key words and concepts

Culture and intercultural

Anyone who has studied culture knows that there is a veritable cornucopia of definitions of this concept. Certainly, I do not need to waste space and time in this essay to debate and discuss those definitions. I have long favored an expansive definition of "culture." The United Nations Educational, Scientific and Cultural Organization's (UNESCO's) definition of culture, as expressed in, for example, the Universal Declaration of Cultural Diversity, says that "culture should be regarded as the set of distinctive spiritual, material, intellectual and emotional features of society or a social group, and that it encompasses, in addition to art and literature, lifestyles, ways of living together, value systems, traditions and beliefs."[3] To my way of thinking, "spiritual," "intellectual and emotional features," "value systems," "traditions and beliefs," in this definition of culture, include religious beliefs, as well as beliefs such as atheism, agnosticism, and secularism.

Logically following this definition of culture, it would imply that when the term "intercultural" is used, it already includes the notion of "inter-religious." Asma Jahangir, the UN Special Rapporteur for Freedom of Religion or Belief, thus rhetorically asked in a 2008 speech to the European Parliament, "Does the term "intercultural" include "Inter-religious?" Her answer: yes.[4] However, in numerous documents of the UN system—as well as by authors—the words "intercultural" and "inter-religious" are often used separately. Why does this happen?

One reason could be that in languages and cultures outside the English-speaking world, the two terms "culture" and "religion" are indeed seen separately. There is little that can be done about that. However, yet another dyad of reasons may be ascribed to the polar positions that are held about religion in the international system by international bureaucrats and political leaders. On the one side may be those who hold that religion has no place in international politics, and by separating out inter-religious and intercultural, intergovernmental organizations can deal with the latter and leave the inter-religious matters to imams, rabbis, priests, and other religious clergy and NGOS. On the other side are those who hold that religion has a special role to play in international politics, and by taking "inter-religious" out of the "intercultural" realm, "inter-religious" receives a privileged position in international discourse. Quite naturally, there may be those who hold positions more in the middle rather than on either pole.

Personally, as in the case of Asma Jahangir, I am inclined to the view that "intercultural" does include "inter-religious." A major effort of the Alliance has been on reducing tensions between the so-called Muslim world and Western world. Of course, the former is defined primarily in terms of religion. The latter is defined in terms of geography and culture. Naturally, the distinctions between the two spheres are not neat and clear-cut, and indeed, some of the conflicts happen because these distinctions are not so definite. For instance, some tensions exist between Muslim immigrants and the host communities in North America and Europe. Sometimes the tensions are less between state and immigrants than between migrant and host communities in these cases. In the fight against Al Qaeda and other terrorist organizations, there is significant collaboration between Western states and members of the Organization of the Islamic Conference (OIC). But the fact remains that first, there are often significant political-philosophical differences between states in the West and member states of the OIC[5]; and second, for the average person on the Muslim or Western street, the perception often is that there is a distinct Western sphere and a distinct Islamic sphere. Here, the Western world may be seen as North America and Europe, and the Islamic world as members of the Organization of the Islamic Conference (although in perception the Muslim world may be seen as the Arab countries and possibly South Asian countries).

What is clear, and what is often demonstrated by polls of populations, is the lack of knowledge and the prevalence of stereotypes in each sphere toward the other sphere. For instance, a Pew poll in 2007 showed that 58 percent of US respondents knew "nothing" or "not very much" about Islam.[6] A Gallup poll in 2009 reported that 63 percent of Americans had "none at all" or "very little knowledge" about Islam.[7] This lack of knowledge is associated with prejudice. As the *Islam and the West: Annual Report on the State of Dialogue* put it, "Where religious literacy is weak, efforts to demonize the 'other' flourish."[8] Thus, people who believe that Muslims oppose equal rights for men and women tend to be much more likely to report prejudice among Muslims, although majorities of Muslims in Iran, Egypt, and Saudi Arabia in other Gallup polls say that women and men should have equal legal rights.[9] Lack of knowledge about the other leads to tensions and violence between Muslims and Westerners, either across countries or within countries. Therefore, the actions of the UN Alliance of Civilizations have a lot to do with building bridges between populations through moving people from situations of ignorance and stereotypes to intercultural (including inter-religious) respect and peace. One potential model of how this could work is offered below.

From tensions and violence to intercultural respect and peace

Why do tensions, polarization, and violence occur between those who occupy different cultural—including religious—identities? At least some of this, as shown in Fig. 1 below, is commonly attributed to ignorance, but I think apathy is also a major issue.[10] Although often commonly linked, we may distinguish between apathy and ignorance about religions in a very simple manner. Apathy is when people do not even care to know about other religions, whereas ignorance is not an individual's fault as much as it is a result of the lack of attention paid by the traditional educators about religions—be they government, clergy, or families—to teach about different religions. It is the combination of apathy and ignorance that leads to the prevalence of stereotypes about other religions and their followers, which contributes to tensions and violence.[11] However, as the dotted line in Fig. 1 shows, ignorance itself can also directly lead to tensions and violence between groups.

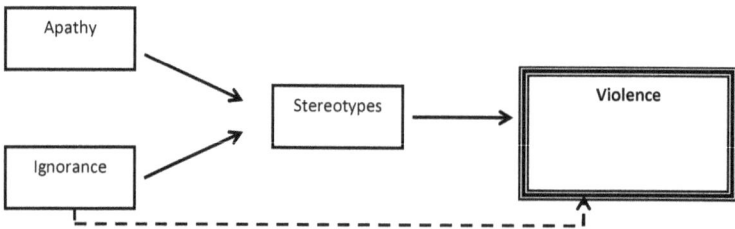

Figure 1. A Path to Intercultural Violence.

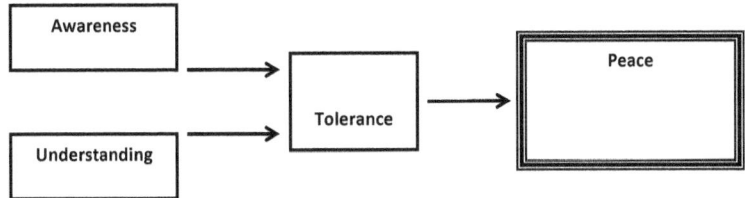

Figure 2. A Path to Intercultural Peace.

How do we move from tensions and violence to respect and peace? My understanding of the steps required is detailed in Fig. 2. Tolerance is often cited as the answer, but it is probably, in my view, merely a way station on the route to the terminus of respect and peace.[12] This is because tolerance does not necessarily mean active acceptance and respect but often grudging acceptance: an attitude that may be described as "yes, I know you're different, and as long as you don't bother me, I don't care." But, even getting to tolerance itself requires awareness and understanding about other cultures—including religions. Awareness relates to knowledge about other religions, while understanding refers to not only knowledge (or the "facts") about religions, but also the contextual underpinnings of religious beliefs and practices followed by particular groups of people. These contextual underpinnings include history, geography, and underlying cultural foundations of the particular groups of people.

While education and media are thus obviously important in raising awareness and understanding, getting from there to tolerance requires inter-faith dialogue and actions. However, inter-faith dialogue and actions will not be enough to get to respect and peace. Getting from tolerance to respect and peace requires domestic and international actors to
1. advocate for the commonality of humanity;
2. build bridges between sectors and actors committed to overcoming differences and establishing peace;
3. catalyze and facilitate the projects that help in the above actions; and
4. disseminate the products of these projects.

As one of the key international actors involved in the complex interplay between intercultural relations and global politics, the UN Alliance of Civilizations has taken some specific steps related to religion, which are detailed below in Part II.

Part II: Actions related to religion undertaken by the alliance of civilizations
In April 2007, Secretary-General Ban Ki-moon appointed Jorge Sampaio, former President of Portugal, as High Representative for the UN Alliance of Civilizations. This marked the beginning of the second phase of the AoC, with the development of an action-oriented implementation plan focusing on initiatives and projects in the areas of youth, media, education, and migration.

The Annual Forums of the Alliance provide an opportunity to engage various sectors—including faith-based organizations—in partnering with the Alliance in the various areas of the Implementation Plan. The First AoC Madrid Forum was hosted by the Government of Spain on January 15–16, 2008; the Second AoC Istanbul Forum was hosted by the Government of Turkey on April 6–7, 2009; and the Third Rio Forum was hosted by the Government of Brazil, May 27–29, 2010. The Forums are high-profile, action-oriented events that bring together a powerful network of political leaders, governments, international organizations, civil society groups, religious communities, as well as media and corporate leaders.

As previously mentioned at the top of this essay, the Alliance clearly recognizes the important role of religion in the creation and reconciliation of divides between people. Accordingly, the Alliance of Civilizations places a strong emphasis on engagement with religious leaders, faith-based organizations, and faith communities toward constructive ends. The Alliance of Civilizations seeks to provide religious leaders with the space to encourage the positive role that religious leaders and communities can play in public debates, often in interaction with politicians and other civil society actors. While religious leaders continue to engage each other in dialogue and have tremendous influence, it is often politicians who make substantive decisions that can create or mitigate conflicts. This means there is a credible need for an interface between religious leaders and politicians. Moreover, while religious leaders and politicians may proclaim the need for peace, it is civil society's "buy-in" that is critical to establishing, maintaining, and resolving conditions that are conducive to peace at the grassroots level. Therefore, the Alliance seeks to draw input from multiple other sectors of society—politicians, media, civil society, youth—as it goes about doing its business of engaging religious leaders and faith-based organizations.

As in the Alliance's work with other sectors of civil society, engaging religious leaders and faith-based communities—as well as organizations interested in issues of religion—in relevant issues is made by the Alliance acting as an advocate, bridge-builder, catalyst, and disseminator. Many of these activities are showcased at the annual Forums. A few examples of this engagement are as follows:

Working with faith-based organizations and other non-governmental partners
The Alliance has established a formal partnership with Religions for Peace, which is the largest international coalition of religious leaders dedicated to promoting peace. At the 2008 Alliance Forum in Madrid, the Alliance co-organized with Religions for Peace a working session bringing together religious leaders from around the world with politicians and civil society leaders to explore ways in which they can support peace-building efforts. A major outcome of Madrid was a joint commitment to active involvement in conflict resolution, reconciliation between different faiths, empowerment of women, and engagement of young people to ensure that they are not swayed by extremist ideologies. At the 2009 Alliance Istanbul Forum, a working breakfast co-organized by Religions for Peace made several concrete recommendations to the Alliance on ways to advance partnerships among religious leaders and groups and intergovernmental organizations, governments, and other actors to resolve conflicts and promote peace and development. This session also featured models of cooperation and examples of multi-religious engagement in peace processes, thus providing participants a valuable opportunity to disseminate their work to a global audience. For instance, Religions for Peace offered a model for cooperation focusing on three core approaches: (1) multi-religious efforts can be more powerful symbolically and substantively than the efforts of individual religious groups acting alone; (2) "representative" multi-religious structures through their leaders, outstanding persons, grassroots congregations, and other organizational manifestations serve as the main agents of multi-religious cooperation; and (3) cooperation on multiple levels, including global, regional, national, and local levels. Among the examples of multi-religious engagement in peace processes shared during the discussion

included examples from Africa, Sri Lanka, and the Middle East. Specific reference was made to the newly established inter-religious council for Middle East and North Africa (*Religions for Peace* MENA). In a press conference the previous day, a bold appeal to Alliance of Civilizations about the situation in Israel and Palestine issued by the *Religions for Peace* MENA was presented. This was seen by the participants as an example of constructive and timely multi-religious advocacy.

The Alliance has also played a role in advancing the Humanitarian Forum, a network of key humanitarian and charitable organizations from across the world whose aim is to help faith-based humanitarian and civil society groups face the new challenges that have emerged in a post-9/11 world.[13] Many faith-based humanitarian organizations, particularly in the Muslim world, are operating in a climate of mistrust and facing difficult funding and operational challenges as a result. The aim of the Humanitarian Forum is to help faith-based charitable and humanitarian groups tackle these challenges by fostering partnerships and closer cooperation. To do that, it aims at supporting capacity building to help improve organizational efficiency and to advocate for a legal framework of greater transparency and accountability to assist social service-oriented Faith-Based Organizations (FBOs) in facing the challenges of a post-9/11 world (for example, indiscriminate freezing of funds). As an example of bringing religious actors together to function effectively, in Kuwait, the Humanitarian Forum brought together all the NGOs that work internationally, both Sunni and Shia to help them share good practice in areas like good governance and financial management.

The Alliance facilitated the creation of an International Network of Foundations in Madrid in 2008. Since then, work has been carried out to identify four areas of common interest: intercultural and inter-religious dialogue, education and translation, arts and media, and the engagement of religious leaders in peace-building efforts. During the Istanbul Forum, a special session of the network of foundations outlined its priority activities moving forward: knowledge exchange, information sharing, and dissemination in the four focus areas; operational support with a view to developing tools that help identify projects and partners and build capacity; identification of collaborative opportunities; and advocacy and contributing to public policy.

Working with and for youth

The UN AoC Youth Program involves work with all types of youth organizations, including faith-based ones. The *Youth Solidarity Fund* (YSF; a competitive mechanism providing seed funding to outstanding youth-led initiatives that promote long-term constructive relationships between young people from diverse cultural and religious backgrounds) allowed the AoC to partner with several youth organizations working on inter-faith issues. For example, a winner of the YSF is GenPeace, a network of organizations and individuals committed to youth-led advocacy for a just and sustainable peace in the Philippines. Their project allowed the delivery of a series of youth leadership training sessions on peace and human rights in Mindanao, in the Southern region of the Philippines. The project aimed at increasing the capacity of youth leaders and at connecting different Muslim, Christian, and Indigenous youth organizations for a more consolidated youth peace advocacy in the Philippines.

Another winner was Pax Romana, which has now produced a final report on its Project, *Listening and Speaking With Respect: Students, Faith and Dialogue,* which can be used as a model for other youth organizations doing similar work.

In addition to this work through the YSF, the UN AoC partners with various faith-based youth organizations or networks of similar organizations such as the Interfaith Youth Core (IFYC), which offers training to their members, supporting advocacy and networking. The UN AoC takes part in their conferences, teams up with them for advocacy regarding the role of youth in intercultural and inter-faith dialogue, and conducts networking and other cooperative actions.

The UN AoC also partners with faith-based organizations with youth focus such as Intersections, which is a multicultural, multi-faith, global initiative of the Collegiate Church of New York, the oldest corporation in North America dating back to 1628. They seek to build respectful relationships among diverse individuals and communities to forge common ground and develop strategies that promote justice, reconciliation, and peace. A portion of their activities are focused on youth. The UN AoC promotes their tools and work on our website and consults them in the design of various UN AoC initiatives in the area of youth.

Building bridges and working to disseminate knowledge and information
The Alliance has also worked with religious leaders and given them a prominent role in the development of its *Rapid Response Media Mechanism* (RRMM) project, which consists of an online resource of experts on issues such as religion, international relations, and globalization who lend their voices and expert commentary to journalists as sensitive issues or events arise. As an example, the Alliance worked closely with religious leaders during the controversy surrounding the anti-Quran film *Fitna*, by far-right Dutch MP Geert Wilders. Specifically, the RRMM project helped generate op-eds from Muslim religious and non-religious leaders appealing for calm (an op-ed co-signed by H.E. Dim Siamsuddin, Prince Hassan of Jordan, and Hamza Yussuf was published in the *International Herald Tribune* and another op-ed by Archbishop Tutu was also published in a number of Arabic newspapers).

The Alliance also facilitates the discussion of issues over reporting about religion, such as a discussion organized at the Istanbul Forum on "Reporting Across Cultural Divides: Global Perspectives." Instead of participants talking past each other in their own separate spaces, this session explored many sensitive issues in the reporting about religious issues that have raised controversy recently. This key role of the Alliance is aimed at negotiating the common ground between the different perspectives of media and media professionals from different backgrounds.

In addition, the media team of the AoC (sometimes with partners) has provided training for journalists and opinion leaders on issues related to perceptions of religion, reporting and writing on religion, and professional development. In 2009–2010, these trainings have taken place in Pakistan, Indonesia, Nepal, the United Kingdom, and Egypt as well as online. Beyond the training, the workshops have the aim to get the journalists to dialogue across their different religious backgrounds, debate contentious issues in private, and produce and disseminate joint news stories.

The *Education about Religions and Beliefs Clearinghouse* (http://www.aocerb.org), formally launched at the Istanbul Forum in April 2009, encompasses learning about the world's diverse religions and beliefs as also ethics education, tolerance education, and civic education. The clearinghouse is motivated by the urgent need to remedy ignorance, reduce stereotypes, and promote knowledge and understanding about the "other"—including the religious "other"—as a way toward respect and peace in society, and create an online community of those who are interested in promoting these objectives. This clearinghouse focuses on the school level in its initial stage. Partners include higher education institutions, intergovernmental organizations, and non-governmental organizations (including faith-based organizations) that have undertaken research or carry out activities in this realm. The ultimate goal of this kind of education, and this clearinghouse, is to provide the knowledge for students to live together. The main sections of the clearinghouse include an overview; resources (guidelines and learning and teaching materials); relevant organizations; a journal; events; a forum; and news that could be useful to teachers, policy-makers, and researchers.

In conjunction with the Council of Europe, the North-South Center, and the Research Centre for Islamic History, Art and Culture, the Alliance has encouraged a project that seeks to discover the interconnections between Muslim and Western civilizations historically and develop appropriate pedagogical techniques to disseminate these connections. The 2009 Istanbul Forum saw the creation of a nascent network for this purpose.

A session at the Istanbul Forum introduced the work developed under the Network of European Foundations (NEF) Initiative on Religion and Democracy in Europe, which focuses on the relationship between religion and democracy in European societies. NEF presented its findings in the specific fields of health and school systems in Europe, and representatives of other regions contributed as discussants. The discussion began with a presentation on the findings of the NEF thematic dossier on the "Teaching about religions in European school systems," including approaches, challenges, and recommendations. Subsequently, the NEF findings on Religion and Healthcare in the European Union were presented. The influence of religion on national healthcare policy and, in particular, the issue of belief-based exemption for health care providers from performing certain duties, and issues related to death, sexual and reproductive health, and mental health were all briefly addressed as well. In the discussion that followed, participants raised several interesting questions including whether religion should be regarded as a liability or as a positive force in health policy; whether certain policy issues are affected by religion as such or rather by culture and traditional cultural practices; and whether the state should provide exemptions to doctors and nurses and within what limits.

Building bridges

In an example of the Alliance's role as a bridge-builder, the premier Marketplace of Ideas event at the 2009 Istanbul Forum featured the world's most exciting, innovative, and lesser known civil society projects, aimed at advancing intercultural understanding, in front of a high-level audience. The goal of the Marketplace was to present grassroots projects that are unique, but also have the potential to be scaled up and replicated in other diverse communities around the world. By bringing these projects to the attention of leaders from governments, international organizations, business, religion, civil society, and academia, the Alliance sought to inspire new thinking about current challenges and to connect some of the world's most dynamic civil society entrepreneurs with an audience of decision-makers who have the ability to give their work greater visibility and impact. To that end, projects were selected for presentation, which did not already possess firmly established links with the UN system and had yet to be truly 'discovered' by the international community. Almost 100 applications were received, from which eighteen projects were selected via a comprehensive review process. Four of these projects had faith components, such as:

1. The 99. A comic based on the ninety-nine attributes of Allah; each of ninety-nine comic book characters is based on one of the ninety-nine attributes. The religion of the characters is not specified, and the positive value or attribute each character represents is inclusive and relevant to every society. (http://www.the99.org)

2. Ramadan Festival. A series of cultural events during Ramadan that is organized in multiple cities around Europe. The festival is aimed at fostering social cohesion and building bridges between Muslims and Non-Muslims.(http://www.ramadanfestival.org)

3. Tools 4 Trialogue. A project that gives young British students an exciting and topical encounter with religious texts from within their own faith and then facilitates discussion with students from other faiths. (http://www.3ff.org.uk/prog_t4t.htm)

4. Pakistan Madrasa Project. A project aiming to reform curricula, improve infrastructure, and offer teacher training at religious schools all

over Pakistan to help strengthen education standards. (http://www.icrd.org)

The Alliance has also participated in a number of initiatives aimed at creating a connection between religious organizations and the political sphere. Among them are the World Congress of religious leaders organized by Kazakhstan over the last five years; King Abdullah's initiative of a Forum of Abrahamic Faiths; and Tony Blair's Faith Foundation. The Kazakhstan congress (the third of which was held in July 2009) convened by the government of Kazakhstan aims to be an "organic and effective global dialogue" between religions and promote "mutual understanding between spiritual leaders, religions, and nations."[14] King Abdullah's initiative has led to meetings in 2008 and 2009 in Madrid and Geneva, respectively.[15] The Tony Blair Faith Foundation has worked actively in the areas of education and social action,[16] and relevant news about education and youth areas from the Foundation is actively posted on the various websites of the Alliance.

Under the "Restore Trust, Rebuild Bridges" initiative, a cluster of projects was jointly developed by the Alliance and partner organizations in the wake of the Gaza crisis in early 2009. This initiative followed a meeting co-organized by the Anna Lindh Foundation and the Alliance of Civilizations in February 2009, aimed at assessing the impact of the crisis in Gaza on relations among and within societies in the Euro-Mediterranean region. Among the several actions proposed to be held is a seminar on Jerusalem as a city of coexistence between monotheistic religions with participants coming from both shores of the Mediterranean.

Concluding challenges and recommendations

Based on the experience of the UN Alliance of Civilizations, one can offer the following observations on the difficulties, recommendations, and ideas for dealing with religious groups.

One difficulty is the absence of mechanisms for effective mutual engagement between and among governments, multilateral organizations promoting fruitful relations, and religious leaders themselves. Although some governments, for instance, have active dealings with religious leaders, others steer clear of such figures. Currently, although religious leaders often meet with leaders of multilateral organizations, there is no body through which each side can regularly convey concerns and issues to each other.

A second area of challenge is the question of "who speaks for my faith" issue. Even in those faiths where there is a leader who is often seen as a representative of the faith—as for example the Pope in the case of Catholicism, or local bishops—there can often be those from the same faith who vigorously dissent from the pronouncements of the leaders. More often than not, identifying leaders of religions that do not have established clergy or hierarchy or are concentrated in a few areas is a task fraught with tension and suspicion.

Third, there is still a great deal of suspicion and resistance in some parts of the world to give a role to religious groups in the public sphere. Although this is widely thought to be an issue in the "secular" developed world, the leadership in the developing world may also have concerns about religious groups, partly because of their fear of a political threat to their regimes and partly also owing to an education and orientation which is more secular.

Fourth, there is a tendency to concentrate on inter-faith dialogue without identifying concrete projects to move beyond dialogue to action. Those who are steeped in religion and theology often are eager to engage in inter-faith dialogue. While this is certainly important in enabling people of different religions to get to know and understand each other, true respect and peace may come only from transcending the inherent differences in faith practices to work together on issues that affect followers of all religions, as well as those who do not practice any religion.

Some recommendations and ideas that may be offered to gather practical benefit from engaging with faith-based groups and religious leaders include the following:

1. Engaging media to raise the visibility of multi-religious dialogue and cooperation in building peace and promoting the common good is vital to changing the public perception of religion.
2. States and political leaders as well as multilateral organizations must look for appropriate frameworks to effectively engage appropriate religious leaders on the common crises confronting humanity whether it is global economic crises or global warming. At the same time, clergy and believers should also be engaged at the local level by local leaders in dealing with issues such as insulting behavior that have the potential to

spark conflict between local communities or issues such as improving education at the local level that involve cooperation for common ends.

3. Involving schools, universities, NGOs, media (both secular and nonsecular), in tandem with religious leaders and families to confront apathy, ignorance, and stereotypes and moving toward awareness, understanding, tolerance, respect, and peace is vital, particularly for young people who will be tomorrow's leaders. This is important not only in confronting apathy, ignorance, and stereotypes in the Western and Muslim worlds, but for people who come from other parts of the world that may become more prominent and omnipresent in the global world of today and tomorrow.

4. Utilize the inherent openness, vibrancy, and technical skills of young people who are religious believers to work toward uncovering and emphasizing what is similar among people rather than what is different. Young people often tend to be curious about what is unfamiliar; they are energetic in discovering differences and similarities and are equipped to use technology to surmount physical, geographical, and religious barriers.

Notes

1. I am indebted to my colleagues at the UN AoC—Emmanuel Kattan, Daanish Masood, and Isabelle Legare—for their input into this piece and to Cecilia Logo-Kofoed for the rendering of Figs 1 and 2. Naturally, views expressed in this article do not necessarily represent their views or those of the Alliance of Civilizations.
2. For details on the AoC and its activities, visit the website http://www.unaoc.org/, and the High Level Group Report calling for the establishment of the Alliance may be found at http://www.unaoc.org/content/view/64/94/lang,english/.
3. See UNESCO Declaration on Cultural Diversity (Paris: UNESCO, 2002), p. 12.
4. The speech was delivered June 18, 2008; for the archived press release of the speech, see http://www.europarl.europa.eu/sides/getDoc.do?language=NL&type=IM-PRESS&reference=20080616IPR31799.
5. Actually, the differences may have more to do with levels of development and education than religion. Thus, for instance, some Muslim states' perspectives on issues such as women's rights, sexual orientation, and freedom of expression and religion are also shared by non-Muslim developing countries.
6. Cited in World Economic Forum, Islam and the West: Annual Report on the State of Dialogue (Geneva: January 2008), p. 72. The report does go on to say that "Reliable data on Muslim knowledge of Christianity or Judaism is more difficult to come by, but similar knowledge gaps may exist there as well."

7. Gallup/The Coexist Foundation, Religious Perceptions in America: With an In-Depth Analysis of U.S. Attitudes Toward Muslims and Islam, available at http://www.muslimwestfacts.com/mwf/125318/Religious-Perceptions-America.aspx (accessed March 10, 2010).

8. World Economic Forum, *Islam and the West: Annual Report on the State of Dialogue* (Geneva: January 2008), p. 73.

9. See Michelle Boorstein, "Americans' bias against Jews, Muslims linked, poll says," *Washington Post* (January 21, 2010), p. A 3.

10. My wife, a high school social studies teacher at a public school, is confronted daily with staggering apathy.

11. For an interesting psychological look at apathy caused by injury and associated with stereotypes, see Bruce L. Miller, Jeffrey L. Cummings, *The Human Frontal Lobes: Functions and Disorders*, (New York: Guilford Press, 2006), p. 15.

12. Relatedly, see Gustav Niebuhr, *Beyond Tolerance: Searching for Interfaith Understanding in America* (New York: Viking Press, 2008), p. 40.

13. More information on the Humanitarian Forum is at http://www.humanitarianforum.org/ (accessed March 18, 2009).

14. More information on this gathering (three of which have been held, the most recent being in 2009) may be found at http://www.religions-congress.org/.

15. For one report on King Abdullah's inter-faith dialogue efforts, see Fahad Alhomoudi, "Saudi Arabia's Push for Religious Dialogue," *Common Ground News Service* (July 21, 2009) accessed March 16, 2010 at http://www.commongroundnews.org/article.php?id=25935&lan=en&sid=1&sp=0.

16. More information about the Tony Blair Faith Foundation may be found at http://www.tonyblairfaithfoundation.org (accessed March 16, 2010).

CROSSCURRENTS

THE UNITED NATIONS DEVELOPMENT PROGRAMME (UNDP) WORKING WITH FAITH REPRESENTATIVES TO ADDRESS CLIMATE CHANGE
The Two Wings of Ethos and Ethics

Natabara Rollosson[1]

On November 3rd, 2009 at Windsor Castle in the United Kingdom, the United Nations Development Programme (UNDP) cohosted a summit that gathered religious and secular leaders from around the world to announce their action-based commitments to protecting the environment and addressing climate change. Religious participants included representatives from numerous traditions from within nine major faiths: Baha'ism, Buddhism, Christianity, Daoism, Hinduism, Judaism, Islam, Sikhism, and Shintoism.

Engaging substantively with the faiths on environment and climate change issues was new to UNDP's work. Even though over the years UNDP had engaged in development projects on different issues that have involved faith-based organizations (FBOs) as partners, it was not until the direct interaction at Windsor that the opportunities of working on climate change with FBOs came into focus.

Instead of bringing religions together to agree upon one collective statement on climate change, the Windsor gathering encouraged each of the faith representatives to develop respective action plans to address environmental issues in their own unique way. As the faiths shared their different approaches, some faiths took note of other plans and openly

---

[1]Natabara Rollosson consults for UNDP on environment and climate change issues and faith partnerships. The opinions expressed in this article belong to the author alone, and are not necessarily reflective of the opinions or positions of UNDP, member states or other UNDP staff.

acknowledged their desire to replicate certain elements of other faiths' action templates. The overall theme of the gathering was a "celebration" of diverse action plans and appreciation for the natural environment, with some faiths inspired to spontaneously transcend and expand their originally conceived commitments.

A month later, in December, a stark contrast played out on the world stage. This time, the Conference of the Parties to the UN Framework Convention on Climate Change brought governments together in Copenhagen. However, delegates came with a notable difference in approach, and one that has plagued nations for decades. The history of climate change negotiations can be characterized as a mentality of *scarcity*: governments generally wanting to do as little as possible while pushing others to do as much as possible.

In an interesting contrast of philosophies, the FBOs came together with an entirely different mentality of *abundance*, saying in effect: "this is what we can offer; this is what we are going to do." They did not say "we'll only do this if another faith does this, or if the government does this."

It was during preliminary religious events and gatherings leading up to Windsor that UN Assistant Secretary-General and UNDP Assistant Administrator Olav Kjørven first noticed the dichotomy of the abundance and scarcity mentalities. Kjørven hypothesized the world's faiths—joined together—could possibly become the planet's largest civil society movement for change: "[W]ith their unparalleled presence throughout the world, the world's religions could be the decisive force that helps tip the scales in favor of a world of climate safety and justice for future generations."

One of UNDP's non-governmental partners, the Alliance of Religions and Conservation (ARC), a secular organization based in the United Kingdom, played the key role in leading on, harnessing, and encouraging the abundance mentality. Prior to the summit, ARC set out to consult directly with faith representatives to support them in building their own action plans, incorporating a methodology that addressed their internal structures and highlighted the inherent strengths of each faith.

Alliance of Religions and Conservation approached the faith representatives with a guide to creating multi-year plans that emphasized seven key areas, through which many of the world's major faith traditions can have significant impact on environmental action through their own resources, traditions, and beliefs. These were as follows:

1. Faith-consistent use of assets: land and forests; construction and buildings; investments (including micro-finance); water; food and hospitality; purchasing and property.
2. Education and young people: curricula; conservation and recycling policy; school buildings and grounds; youth camps and nature retreats.
3. Pastoral care: theological education and training; liturgies and quotations; sacred places; rediscovering past traditions and wisdom; crisis and climate change adaptation.
4. Lifestyles: environmental audits; simple living traditions; families; pilgrimage and tourism; combined purchasing power.
5. Media and advocacy: internal and external subject matter; circulation and influence.
6. Partnerships & eco-twinning: links to other groups and projects in other parts of the world; establishing dedicated staff; involving lay people.
7. Celebration: new and traditional festivals; introducing new practices; celebrating sacred spaces.

Through a consultation process, the FBOs and religious leaders involved delved into their traditions to find their link with the environment and inherent commitment to preserve and nurture the natural world. For many, it was a dusting off and rediscovery of their core religious values concerning creation, but now with new meaning and relevance in the context of today's global environmental crisis. The FBOs were emboldened to recognize and catalyze their unique role to play.

An overarching theme in the development of each of the plans was the emergence of *ethos* in addition to ethics, which is where the faiths of the world may have a significant role to play in addressing climate change and environmental protection. Where secular entities and governments seek to build consensus, legislate, and regulate to address a crisis, the faiths seek to inspire and instill the deeper values that motivate right action. Ethics set boundaries for behavior in an effort to establish and maintain justice. Concomitantly, ethos inspires just behavior. Together ethos and ethics are essential to motivate proper action.

Signs are showing that when addressing climate change, the traditional governmental approach through ethics may need to also employ the influence of ethos. The different outcomes of the Windsor and Copenhagen gatherings tell an important tale: in one, communities were stepping into partnerships across national boundaries and into plans of action; the other appeared mired in disagreement. One adopted the reactive stance of political posturing and gamesmanship, while another adopted a proactive approach of attempting to lead by example.

At Windsor, the FBOs and religious leaders were invited to come with commitments to action plans. The atmosphere was in no way encouraged to be competitive. Instead, it created the space for review of original action plans as a result of listening to other presentations. Many FBOs arrived at the summit in Windsor already having achieved a number of goals. All together, over thirty new multi-year plans were launched.

Examples from the action plans include some Daoist temples in China converting to solar power and some Hindu and Muslim communities creating faith-based eco-labeling systems. Also included across the various faith traditions were plans for developing ethical investment policies; greening different religious buildings; protecting sacred forests; printing sacred books on environmentally friendly paper; creating and providing relevant educational programs through various religious fora.

The FBOs and religious leaders drew upon their virtues, many of which were shared, such as their sense of service, mindfulness and overall respect for the natural world as a *living planet* to be cherished, protected, and nurtured. This attitude is already different from governments' emblematic economic view of the natural world as a resource to be managed. Faith leaders always kept this in the forefront of their thinking and planning, leading to the development of action plans to achieve what they felt was right and just for them, with an added value offering a positive example for others. ARC often cited an apt quote during the preliminary consultations with the faiths, which came from a Confucian saying "First practice what you want to preach; then preach about what you already practice."

The FBOs and religious leaders gathered to announce their achievements and commitments in the historic Windsor Castle in the United Kingdom. The event was cohosted by HRH Prince Philip and United

Nations Secretary-General Ban Ki-moon. A number of secular leaders specializing in the environment and sustainable investment also attended, exploring new partnerships with the faiths to support their multi-year plans. In his keynote address, Secretary-General Ban commended the gathered faith representatives thus:

> Political leaders must understand that the public expects action—action now. Faith communities can help communicate this message.... You can inspire, you can provoke, you can challenge your political leaders, through your wisdom, through your power, through your followers. Together let us walk toward a more sustainable path, one that respects our planet, and provides a safer, healthier, more equitable future for all of us.

Global media coverage of the Windsor event was extensive, and for many media outlets, it was the first time to cover the role of religions in the context of climate change and the environment. The coverage served to reaffirm the internal efforts of those managing the action plans within each of the faiths. The news highlighting the achievements and commitments by the faith representatives served as inspiring examples for other faith representatives and governments around the world.

The following December in Copenhagen, the governmental meeting did not mirror the same spirit of commitment that the faith representatives demonstrated in Windsor. And the outcomes reflect this. To ensure more encouraging results in future negotiations, it may be that deeper values and inspired commitments are needed. For governments, striving to reach consensus on an international treaty on climate change is challenging indeed, and they must not give up in the efforts to reach an agreement that is comprehensive, equitable, balanced, and binding. However, some FBOs and religious leaders clearly can offer valuable lessons in the abundance mentality, and setting positive examples of action, instead of the scarcity mentality of unwillingness and political competition.

Being among the oldest and most enduring of institutions, the world's faith communities exemplify social sustainability, specializing in the ability to influence long-term generational change. With the immediate global need for transformational change, the faiths have an essential role to play. UNDP experienced firsthand how the faiths can be engaged as valuable partners in addressing climate change and inspiring the empowering values needed to guide such essential action.

United Nations Development Programme is now looking into how its global presence through over 130 Country Offices can reach out to its like-minded partners in the faith-based world, in its work on achieving environmental sustainability. Ways are being explored at the country level to work with faiths to provide support and guidance for their multi-year plans, enabling practical steps that could help societies to shift toward a low-carbon future.

By setting substantive environmental commitments, achieving goals and setting an example for their followers and particularly their youth, the world's faith leaders provide important assets and harness critical opportunities. They can catalyze the far-reaching proactive change that is necessary to work in support of the secular efforts to develop the regulatory framework to address climate change and provide environmental protection and regeneration that the living planet urgently needs. As governments struggle with the sails of climate ethics and justice, the ethos of religions may provide the winds needed to arrive at the destination.

Some highlights of commitments made by faith representatives
A selection of faith commitments and achievements is excerpted from the summary publication *Many Heavens, One Earth—Faith Commitments to Protect the Living Planet*, which can be downloaded from the Windsor2009.org website.

Faith-consistent use of assets

Construction and existing buildings
Daoists in China are installing solar panels in Daoist temples throughout China. The first Daoist ecological temple—at Taibaishan in Shaanxi Province—was built in 2007 with local sustainable materials and is now a model for ecological temples being planned throughout China.

Land and forests
The Northern Diocese of the Evangelical Lutheran Church of Tanzania is implementing an intensive tree planting campaign, with 8.5 million

trees to create community forests across the region, at a cost of US$2.5 million, of which two thirds will be raised locally.

Water
The Foundation for Revitalization of Local Health Traditions in Bangalore, India, recently investigated traditional Hindu Ayurvedic teachings that instruct householders "to store water in copper pots." Scientists found that 99 percent of E. coli bacteria are killed within twelve hours of being placed into water stored in copper pots. Some four million under-fives die from diarrhea every year; many from E. coli-related infections. The Sikh plan includes recommending that their gurdwaras—temples—use copper pots for storing water.

Food, hospitality, and retail outlets
In 2005, the managers of the Methodist International Centre—which combines a boutique hotel in London with hostel accommodation for students from around the world—was asked a simple question: why aren't your eggs free range? This led to internal discussions about living one's ethics, and the Centre is now a model of ethical and environmentally conscious sourcing—and is training other religious caterers to do the same.

Financial investments and micro-finance
With Catholics comprising approximately 25 percent of the U.S. population, the U.S. Catholic Coalition on Climate Change is working with its 18,000 parishes, 8,500 schools, four colleges and universities, and dozens of hospitals to link with the U.S. government's Energy Star program to buy green energy, and is initiating conversations with treasurers of Catholic institutions to discuss how Catholic investment portfolios can encourage green energy technology and support environmentally careful companies.

Education and young people

School curricula
In 2006 alone, a quarter of a million Baha'is participated in study circles, devotional meetings, and school classes on the environment. Such

courses, and the acts of service associated with them, are seen to "represent a significant transformative process for Baha'i communities worldwide." The environment is the focus for the next five years of all such Baha'i education initiatives.

Informal education
The Australian Catholic Bishops' Conference is actively practicing green living, gardening, and food in all its schools and places of education. "We encourage all to develop their ecological vocation," and introduce the concept of "an ecological conversion."

Conservation
In 2000, the Maronite Church in Lebanon made its portion of the fragile and precious Harissa forest into a Maronite-Protected Area. The town of Jounieh and three landowners all voluntarily joined the scheme, foregoing considerable money that would be offered by developers. When asked why he had made that decision, one of the landowners said that he remembered back to when he was a boy and had gone for a camping holiday in the forest that was organized by the church. "It was one of the happiest times of my life," he said. "That's why I want to protect the forest now."

Recycling policy
The EcoSikh Plan urges all Sikh *gurdwaras*—temples that feed thirty million people every day in India, regardless of creed or need—to recycle, compost, use green energy, use eco-stoves, start rainwater harvesting, purchase reusable plates and cups, and host open gurdwaras to invite people in from the community to see their green practices.

Environmental monitoring
Religious Organizations Along the River (ROAR), initiated in 1996, is a network of religious congregations and organizations—including many Catholic Sisters—with property in the Hudson Valley of New York State. Their mission is to protect the Hudson River, through advocacy, networking, education, sustainable practices, and simply inspiring people to appreciate it, know it, and monitor it. This movement is

inspired by the Catholic Bishops of the dioceses that span the Columbia River along the western seaboard of the United States who realized in the 1980s that their precious waterway was becoming polluted. They encouraged their faithful to monitor the river and feed that information back at all levels to the state government, to the polluting companies and to the communities.

Pastoral care

Training

The Regeneration Project, which runs Interfaith Power and Light in the United States, has a vision of clergy being "visible and influential leaders in the effort to address global warning" and that "congregations are seen as an integral part of the solution."

Crisis and adaptation

Quaker Peace and Social Witness plans to establish a Sustainability and Peace program exploring the links between conflict and climate change. It is exploring a joint project with its Quaker UN office in Geneva to facilitate and support an interfaith dialog on climate-induced migration.

Liturgies, quotations, and orders of prayer

Many Orthodox Churches have recently developed new liturgies to celebrate their Feast of Creation on September 1st. These new prayers and hymns reinforce the special role Orthodox Christianity gives, not just to protecting creation, but also to blessing it and nurturing it to further fruition. Protestants and Catholics around the world have adopted this concept, and are now beginning to celebrate "Creation Time" from September 1 to St Francis' Feast Day on October 4—a period that for many in the northern hemisphere is also harvest-tide.

Sacred places and sanctuaries

Churchyards, cemeteries, and gardens beside temples and mosques are often rare wild sanctuaries in big cities. Some groups are allowing wilderness areas to grow unabated—through reducing mowing and pesticides—and are producing educational material to remind visitors what natural wonders present in their local area. For example, the ancient trees in the Eyup mosque in Istanbul are the last surviving breeding places for storks on the Golden Horn. Many of the faith plans have this aspect of care built into them, including the Armenian Orthodox, Daoists, Hindus, and Muslims.

Theology of nature, land, forests, water

As part of the development of the Shinto Plan to help create Religious Forestry Standards for forest owning faiths, a program to create in each faith such a theology is being undertaken. In China, the Government of Shaanxi Province is offering to help fund an international conference at which these theologies will be presented.

Stories and practices

The Jewish Plan suggests recovering the ecological value of Shabbat, the Sabbath, as "a day to step back from shopping, manufacturing, flying, driving and technological manipulation of the work...we need to develop ways for Jews who currently observe Shabbat to deepen their sense of its ecological significance, and for Jews who don't currently keep Shabbat in a halakhic sense to explore aspects of Shabbat observance, as an ecological value."

Lifestyles

Green audits

A significant feature of most long-term plans is a commitment not only to audit their buildings, gardens, farmlands, and energy use but also to create eco-model places of worship.

Pilgrimage

The newly formed Muslim Association for Climate Change Action (MACCA) developed a plan to work toward a green Hajj, with the Saudi Minister of the Hajj. The aim is to have the Hajj free of plastic bottles after two years and to introduce initiatives over the next ten years to transform this most important pilgrimage into one that is recognized as environmentally friendly. The vision is that pilgrims will take an understanding of care of creation as an act of faithfulness.

Tourism

In September 2007, the Vatican's Pontifical Council for the Pastoral Care of Migrants and Itinerant People noted that tourism contributes to global warming, if only through the sheer movement of one billion people a year. It urged pilgrims and tourists to remember Genesis 1, in which *"the earth is a garden, a place in which creatures praise the love of Him who created them and where equilibrium is the norm"* and that as tourists they can choose between being for or against the planet. "Perhaps we can travel on foot, opt for hotels and hospitality facilities that are closer to nature, and carry less luggage, so that means of transport emit less carbon dioxide... We can also eat more 'eco-friendly' meals, plant trees to neutralize the polluting effects of our journeys, choose local handicrafts rather than more costly and poisonous items and make use of recyclable and biodegradable materials."

Purchasing power

In 2004, the green New York Jewish organization Hazon launched a Community-Supported Agriculture program called Tuv Ha'Aretz. It involves a synagogue entering a partnership with a local organic farmer and committing to pre-purchase a share of the season's produce. For the farmer, this guarantees a market; for members, this gives access to fresh, organic produce at affordable prices. In the wider context, it helps to preserve farmland, build community, and protect wildlife and water systems from pesticides. By 2009, there were thirty-two Tuv Ha'Artez locations in the United States and Israel, putting more than US$1 million of Jewish purchasing power behind organic farms. One member of Tuv Ha'Aretz was Rahm Emanuel, now chief of staff to Barack Obama, President of the United States.

Media and advocacy

United States'–based *GreenFaith* is creating and developing online and distance education capacities for ordained faith leaders to integrate their experience of the sacred in nature into their teaching, public speaking, spiritual life, and pastoral care. It is doing this through web-based videos (including the popular *Story of Stuff*), consumption resources, and a major web portal currently being planned.

Partnerships, eco-twinning, funding

Dedicated staff, and a dedicated funding source

Buddhists in Cambodia have set up their own environmental organization—Association of Buddhists for the Environment. It is staffed and run by monks and assisted by many secular agencies in reforestation, environmental education, and sustainable housing. At first, it seemed expensive and time consuming to create an office, but the Cambodian Patriarch has realized it is an important element of reaching out to young people. Living their faith in this way has required new skills—making documentaries and websites—as well as old skills like growing and caring for trees. It has also involved rethinking old traditions creatively, including holding ceremonies to ordain trees—as they ordain new monks—to encourage people to protect them.

Eco-twinning & partnerships

The New Psalmist Baptist Church in Baltimore, Maryland, has partnered with one mega church in the slums of Nairobi, Kenya with a network of 2,000 churches in Africa, and another of seventy or more mega churches in the United States. This combined network has fostered water and sanitation projects in Africa. Overall both congregations support seventeen schools, and have created partnerships with environmental entrepreneurs, providing solar-powered water purifiers and sanitation equipment to the Kenyan slums.

Celebration

Traditional & new festivals and platforms

The Northern Diocese of the Evangelical Lutheran Church of Tanzania now has a program of tree planting linked to key life events. For example, trees are presented to children at their baptism, for their parents to plant. Those children in turn must plant a number of their own trees before they can be confirmed. Women also have started campaigns to grow trees, seeking to imitate the famous Wangari Maathai of Kenya in tree planting.

Epilogue

Of special note, the Windsor summit reaffirmed the growing realization that the world's faith communities share the same inherent goal of the UN to protect and provide for the disadvantaged and vulnerable people in the world but now in the newer context of adaptation to climate change. This was seen in the increasing number of *eco-twinning* projects, where faiths in developed countries partner and provide resources for projects in the developing countries, many of which are in Africa. Especially for populations in many developing countries, the effects of climate change are real and pressing. The eco-twinning model encourages those in the developed world to feel a connection and assist those struggling to adapt to the effects of climate change firsthand.

CROSSCURRENTS

THE UNITED NATIONS POPULATION FUND'S (UNFPA'S) LEGACY OF ENGAGING FAITH-BASED ORGANIZATIONS AS CULTURAL AGENTS OF CHANGE

Azza Karam[1]

Introduction—What Is UNFPA?

UNFPA, the United Nations Population Fund, is an international development agency that promotes the right of every woman, man, and child to enjoy a life of health and equal opportunity. UNFPA's mission statement is to support countries in using population data for policies and programs to reduce poverty and to ensure that every pregnancy is wanted, every birth is safe, every young person is free of HIV/AIDS, and every girl and woman is treated with dignity and respect.

Thus, UNFPA helps governments, at their request, to formulate policies and strategies to reduce poverty and support sustainable development. The Fund also assists countries to collect and analyze population data that can help them understand population trends. And it encourages governments to take into account the needs of future generations, as well as those alive today.

The close links between sustainable development and reproductive health and gender equality, the other main areas of UNFPA's work, were affirmed at the 1994 International Conference on Population and Development (ICPD) in Cairo. UNFPA is guided in its work by the Programme of Action (PoA) adopted there. At the conference, 179 countries agreed

that meeting needs for education and health, including reproductive health, is a prerequisite for sustainable development over the longer term. They also agreed on a roadmap for progress with the following goals:
1. Universal access to reproductive health services by 2015.
2. Universal primary education and closing the gender gap in education by 2015.
3. Reducing maternal mortality by 75 percent by 2015.
4. Reducing infant mortality.
5. Increasing life expectancy.
6. Reducing HIV infection rates.

UNFPA maintains that reaching the goals of the PoA of the ICPD is also essential for achieving the Millennium Development Goals (MDGs). These eight goals, which are fully aligned with the ICPD roadmap, have the overarching aim of reducing extreme poverty by half by 2015. UNFPA therefore brings its special expertise in reproductive health and population issues to the worldwide collaborative effort of meeting the MDGs.

This article will outline why UNFPA came to deal with faith-based organizations (FBOs), how it does so as a matter of principles and policy—providing some examples of this work—and will conclude with a few lessons learned and recommendations.

The specificity of UNFPA

As a means of understanding UNFPA's working modality, it is important to highlight five unique aspects of the Fund and its work:
1. UNFPA is the only UN body that provides a comprehensive package of services simultaneously, for and about reproductive health as well as broader population dynamics (e.g., census and data for development, urbanization, migration, disability care, and elderly welfare). This is a critical part of its mandate and distinguishes it from other international agencies working on various specific aspects of health, gender or statistics, and information gathering. This mandate can be described as one that covers human welfare from before conception to the moment of passing. And as vast a responsibility as this is, the Fund is actually one of the "smaller" agencies/bodies within the UN system, relative to financial and human resources.

2. With such a mandate, UNFPA has effectively been given the task of implementing some of the goals that touch on the most sensitive and intimate spheres of human existence, including reproductive health and rights, with all the incumbent baggage of gender relations and gendered identities, sexuality, and related population issues. This means that whether it is counting people, or making everyone count, UNFPA has to deal with many cultural and social taboos, intricately connected to political and economic challenges.

3. UNFPA has emerged as the only UN agency that has invested in systematically developing, training, and successfully testing a unique three-pronged programming methodology: combining gender equality, cultural sensitivity, and the human rights-based approach to programming.[2] These "integrated development approach" trainings have been carried out as pilots at various regional levels with and for UNFPA staff and have been provided to entire UN Country Teams (i.e., beyond UNFPA and inclusive of other UN agencies at the country level), specifically in Bangladesh, Brazil, Iran, Iraq, Jordan, and Macedonia over the course of 2007-2008.

4. Furthermore, UNFPA's work on, for, and with FBOs is grounded in its commitment to acknowledging and proactively *integrating culture into development processes.* Culture, defined by UNFPA as the dynamics which both influence and are impacted upon by the way people think, believe, and behave,[3] is acknowledged by the Fund to be a key feature of human development. Changing attitudes, behaviors, and laws—especially those dealing with gender relations and reproductive health—has proven to be a long-term and complex task. And changing mind-sets can be more difficult than providing services. This has been proven, time and again, to be especially true when lives are bound by centuries-old traditions and complex cultural constructs, in ever changing political contexts.

5. Last but by no means least in this section, UNFPA is the only United Nations agency that has invested—systematically since 2002—in setting up a Global Interfaith Network for Population and Development, with five regional offshoots. The Interfaith Network, with over 250 registered FBOs in a Directory made available to all development partners, is also a forum for sharing of news and information, and its worldwide members act informally to provide UNFPA with advice and guidance as to emerging issues, advocacy, and service delivery needs.

Culture matters...

UNFPA's work on culture has benefited exclusively from experiences documented by *at least* seventy-five of its 112 Country and Regional Offices. Each experience of engaging with cultural agents of change, and accepting the inevitability of cultural dynamics as key to positive social, political, economic, and legal transformation, affirms what the Fund strongly maintains: that *for any process of human development to be sustainable and effective, it has to be aspired to, driven toward, and established, from within.*

That is why the Fund launched, in 2002, its initiative to systematically mainstream culturally sensitive approaches into programming efforts. On the ground, this demands a greater emphasis on working with communities and local agents of change—engaging in dialogue, listening, sharing knowledge and insights, and jointly planning the way to move ahead.

It requires understanding the cultural dynamics in each society where UNFPA works and the positive, as well as the challenging cultural values, assets, expressions and power structures. This effectively translates into working with FBOs, indigenous communities, and other community-based structures as partners in development and human rights.

To aid in the practical programming, UNFPA developed and promotes a tool—"the Culture Lens."[4] The Lens is an analytical and programming tool that helps policy makers and development practitioners analyze, understand, and utilize positive cultural values, assets, and structures in their planning and programming processes, so as to reduce resistance to the ICPD PoA, strengthen programming effectiveness, and create conditions for ownership and sustainability of UNFPA programs, especially in the areas of women's empowerment and promotion of reproductive health and rights.

UNFPA has learned that it "needs to identify, engage and partner with local power structures and religious institutions to strengthen alliances and partnerships....There are many reasons for working with religious and faith based organizations: They have access to people, they live in the community, have legitimacy and credibility among the people who listen to them and seek their advice and counsel, have strong structures and outreach programs, and have institutional, human and financial resources."[5]

The engagement of these partners in addressing reproductive health and gender issues has gone beyond changing individual attitudes and behaviors. It has also placed reproductive health and rights issues on the agenda of many religious organizations, and discussions once considered taboo have been moved into the public arena. For example, family size, early marriage, violence against women, wife inheritance, female genital mutilation and cutting, and reproductive services and rights are now being discussed openly, from the pulpits of a village church, mosque, or temple.[6]

Lessons learned from working from within cultures

In the decade since the ICPD, UNFPA has initiated culturally sensitive approaches in diverse cultural and social contexts. Through this work, a number of common themes have emerged. For example, the Fund has learned that:

Communities can be encouraged to incorporate universally recognized rights into their own realities through an exploration of how human rights and gender issues contribute to the well-being of men, women, children, and families.

Promoting behavior change often begins by identifying individuals who have the capacity and legitimacy to motivate and mobilize communities. Partnering with local "agents of change" has become an invaluable strategy in gaining wider acceptance and ownership of programs.

Effective negotiation requires an understanding of the interests of diverse stakeholders—from political leaders to civil society organizations, cultural leaders, and the private sector. Until their interests are clearly understood, it will be difficult to find common ground.

Gaining the support of agents of change and local power structures is often necessary before engaging effectively with communities. One way to do this is by presenting evidence-based data on issues of concern to the community, such as the health of mothers and children, the impact of violence against women, and the prevalence of HIV/AIDS. Such information can help defuse potential tensions by focusing on the shared goal of people's well-being. Once trust develops, discussions have then expanded to more sensitive issues.

Avoiding value-laden language can help create neutral ground in which understanding and support for program objectives become possible. Just as *carefully developed advocacy campaigns*, closely tailored to the cultural context in which they are launched, make it easier to deal with sensitive subjects. These campaigns, when they reflect a clear understanding of the views of both allies and potential adversaries, and draw from sources that are popular within a given culture, have proven to be effective communication tools that support national processes. In Muslim contexts, using Islamic references in advocacy campaigns has helped to dispel suspicions and promote local ownership, just as working with faith-based leaders across the Christian communities has provided a means to counter stigma and discrimination among people living with HIV in many contexts.

The case for FBOs...
The case for working with FBOs, as one community among many agents of change, is no longer a matter of discussion, but rather one of considered, systematic, and deliberate engagement of like-minded partners. There is clearly an important parallel faith-based universe of development, one that provides an average of 30 percent of health care and educational services in many developing countries, with these figures rising significantly in contexts of conflict and natural disasters. UNFPA acknowledges that "at a time when basic needs are becoming increasingly harder to provide for more than half of the world's population, we can no longer avoid acknowledging these parallel faith-based development interventions which reach so many and provide so much. Many are critical venues for outreach, resources, and service delivery."[7]

UNFPA recognizes that the world of faith-based development organizations is filled with a diversity of mandates, missions, expertise, services, and modality of work, among other things. Similarly, the Fund has had to acknowledge that religions themselves are a vast and complex tapestry, as is reflected in the plurality of FBOs. Among this world are friends of the MDGs and the ICPD. And it is to these friends—with a legacy of engagement and service provision—that the Fund turns to—and views as part of wider civil society partners.

UNFPA's definition of FBOs refers to faith-based or faith-inspired, legally registered non-profit/non-governmental organizations, which are working to deliver a range of services in and around the ICPD areas—

in a manner that is in line with the human rights mandate of the United Nations. It is important to note that several of UNFPA's Offices in the field have engaged with religious leaders (of congregations and heads of religious institutions proper) as a means of "working with the faith-based communities." Increasingly, however, the Fund is advised to distinguish between religious leaders and human rights-oriented FBOs with a track record of delivering services that can be traced, monitored, and evaluated, as per any non-governmental institutional partnership.

The legacy of engaging FBOs as cultural agents actually began in the 1970s with the partnership between the Fund and the University of Al-Azhar in Egypt (Sunni Islam's foremost academic and religious authority) to set up the International Centre for Reproductive Health and Population Studies. Since then, the partnerships have evolved in different countries, with the specific aim of reaching out to constituencies which have, arguably, the most impact in changing the mind-sets of the larger population. Much of this outreach was carried out on the premise that religious communities were therefore critical agents of change, and a great deal was accomplished through these partnerships, as mapped and showcased in UNFPA's seminal publication entitled *Culture Matters: A Legacy of Engaging Faith-Based Organizations* (UNFPA: 2008).

Much of this work since the 1970s, however, was ad hoc and rarely documented, evaluated, or indeed, framed within a policy context. Systematization of such outreach, the provision of training and guidelines to all staff at UNFPA and sister UN agencies through select UN Country Teams, only occurred with the advent of Ms. Thoraya Ahmed Obaid as Under-Secretary General of the United Nations, and Executive Director of UNFPA. As Executive Director, Ms. Obaid steered the Fund toward a much more comprehensive appreciation—conceptually and programmatically—of the domain of cultures, and how they impact gender relations and, ultimately, the realization of the Fund's human rights mandate. Located within this developmental approach is the unique cultural agency of FBOs.

For UNFPA, therefore, this engagement is viewed as part of its overall strategy to create a supportive socio-cultural environment wherein reproductive health and rights, as well as population dynamics, can be effectively realized.

UNFPA's principles of partnership with FBOs

In its *Guidelines for Engaging FBOs as Cultural Agents of Change*, specific mention is made of how the Fund is guided by the following five principles and policy considerations:

1. *Strategic issue-based alliances*: Focusing on the common ground (instead of divisive aspects) allows consideration of joint efforts to achieve the ultimate objectives captured in UNFPA's mission statement. This is realistic when focusing on specific issues. The common ground is a critical building block of these partnerships. UNFPA has found that leaders of faith- and inter-FBOs are open to discussing reproductive health, if issues are addressed with care and sensitivity. It is clear that women's equal rights, and reproductive rights in particular, are not usually the issues that generate consensus among religious leaders—and especially not publicly. Nevertheless, UNFPA recognizes the importance of rallying those within the faith-based communities who are already supportive of the common goals and targets embodied in the ICPD PoA and are reflected in and reindorsed by the MDGs, and have ongoing programs to that effect. One effective approach is to use scientific evidence, on issues such as infant and maternal mortality, violence against women, and HIV and AIDS prevalence rates, for instance, to tap into ethical positions.

Moreover, none of these alliances are required to be lifelong partnerships. Each engagement is predicated upon certain circumstances and needs, and may well be time-bound. This is a valid and necessary aspect of any strategic alliance, which also requires at least anticipating a mutually respectful and agreed-upon exit strategy.

2. *A level playing field:* While UNFPA recognizes the differences between its mandate and approach and those of FBOs, it nevertheless seeks to cooperate as equal partners, depending on each other's comparative advantage and respective strengths. Partnering as equals also entails that neither side is utilized or instrumentalized, but both are relevant agents of action based on their different, and in many instances, complementary strengths. While the partnerships sought within the FBO community are expected to share the objectives of the ICPD-linked MDGs, UNFPA respects that they would reach these objectives differently—using their own language, networks, and *modus operandi*. And in the meantime,

UNFPA acknowledges that the diverse languages and methods require mutual understanding and sensitivity at all times.

3. *Diversity of outreach*: UNFPA ensures that its outreach is multi-faith and balanced according to the religious diversity within communities, nations, and globally. This is often made explicit in the terms of reference of the programs. One of the lessons learned is that this multi-faith outreach approach cannot be implicit. UNFPA also recognizes that to identify like-minded partners and continuously enhance the working modality and program delivery, working with already established multi-faith organizations and communities that already work on an inter- and intra-faith basis is critical.

4. *Clarity, accountability, and consistency*: As with any other partnership, UNFPA sets out clearly (in Memoranda of Understanding, joint proposals, or other project documents) the concrete outcomes expected of the joint endeavors. How the partnership falls within the parameters of its own Strategic Plan defines joint mechanisms of accountability, monitoring, and evaluation. Moreover, the engagement with FBOs needs to be consistent, not a one-off, event-oriented alliance that creates false expectations. An engagement that is designed with a collective sense of ownership and responsibility for specific outcomes in mind is also one that is sustainable. Together, clarity, accountability, and consistency are essential for building the trust necessary to establish a legacy of realistic partnerships.

5. Throughout these partnerships, UNFPA maintains two important dimensions *and* targets of its commitment that significantly enrich the experience and inform its policy considerations:

5.1. *South-South engagement*: Within each region, and among its five regions (e.g., Africa, Arab States, Asia and Pacific, Eastern Europe and Central Asia, and Latin America and the Caribbean), there is much scope for knowledge sharing, creation of knowledge networks, and the strengthening of alliances. Indeed, several UNFPA Country Offices expressed an interest in learning from other experiences of engaging FBOs and indeed, in strengthening their own networks of faith-based partners.

5.2. *Global perspectives, comparisons, and continuity*: There is much to be said for a continuous feedback loop where the national, regional, and the global/international enrich one another. Such knowledge and comparison of engagements at the national, regional and international levels, i.e., feedback loops, enable better appreciation of FBO interventions as well as UNFPA strategies, as well as grounding and sustainability of the partnerships formed.

Examples of partnerships with FBOs

An important realization from the mapping of FBO engagement undertaken by UNFPA from 2006–2008 is that even where headquarters can be too hesitant to engage with the faith-based sectors, some of the country or field-based offices have performed so anyway. This was a natural evolution not necessarily always mandated by policy, but in most instances, because the realities on the ground required it, and it was strategic to realize the developmental objectives.

Following is a select, non-exhaustive list of specific examples to illustrate how UNFPA's culturally sensitive approach has been translated into programmatically engaging FBOs, per region:

Africa

In Mauritania, UNFPA supported scaling-up of a grassroots initiative by the Mauritanian Midwives Association to combat sexual violence against women, bringing it to national scale in collaboration with the government. The initiative yielded significant results, including reports of reduced incidences of rape, increased reporting, and improved responses by the police and community, in addition to incorporation of a component on sexual violence against women and children in the annual work plan of each ministry.

Key to this success was working with religious leaders who were known to be progressive and flexible, and who viewed the endeavor as humanitarian and in line with Islamic principles of helping those who are suffering and vulnerable.

Similarly in Rwanda, UNFPA sensitized members of Protestant, Catholic, and Islamic religious groups, known as Religions Against AIDS, to raise awareness on gender, sexual, and reproductive health and rights. UNFPA also facilitated couples' communication on family planning, HIV/AIDS, and VCT (voluntary counseling and testing).

UNFPA is supporting faith-based partners and local groups of young people in Sierra Leone, by providing reproductive health services, basic health care, psychosocial support and counseling, HIV prevention education, occupational training, and skills development. UNFPA used HIV prevention and promotion of reproductive health as a tool of social cohesion and reconstruction among ex-combatant youth. The Fund also organized its reproductive health awareness–raising sessions within the largest women-attended church in Free Town.

Latin America and the Caribbean
UNFPA supported Alianza Evangelica de Guatemala, a coalition consisting of over 85 percent of the Evangelical Churches in the country, in organizing 200 teams of trainers from the church communities. Trainees included pastors and church leaders, while the training emphasized themes of prenatal care, family planning, and parenting.

In Honduras, UNFPA worked together with FBOs to establish an "Inter-ecclesiastical Committee on HIV/AIDS Prevention," comprised of members from the Catholic, Evangelical, Episcopal, and Adventist churches, as well as the Ministry of Health. The committee meets regularly to jointly strategize on common visions and activities in approaching HIV/AIDS prevention from a religious perspective.

Arab region
Working with Government as well as the Al-Azhar University's International Islamic Center for Population Studies and Research in Egypt, UNFPA supported a project that included 14 traveling seminars for young scholars, on maternal mortality, HIV/AIDS prevention, and women's empowerment, including the importance of girls' education.

In Jordan, UNFPA-sponsored study tours for religious leaders to visit Egypt, to learn about family planning initiatives there. Lectures were also given throughout mosques in Jordan on the topic of gender equality.

Other activities under the initiative included a safe motherhood study tour to Tunisia and the sponsorship of a youth club, which focused on reproductive health peer education.

Eastern Europe and Central Asia
UNFPA worked with the State commission on Religious Affairs, Clerical Department of Muslims, and Mutakalim (a Muslim women's NGO) in

Kyrgyzstan to sponsor a national conference and round tables for religious leaders and NGOs, on various issues related to reproductive health, including family planning, gender equality, and importance of male involvement in all of these aspects. As a result, an official appeal was issued to address the people of Kyrgyzstan emphasizing the significance of promoting reproductive health, family planning, and HIV prevention. This partnership also spurred the creation of a book called "Family Planning in the Legacy of Islam."

In Tajikistan, UNFPA worked with the Islamic University of Tajikistan to assist in implementing family planning and education about sexually transmitted infections (including HIV/AIDS) into the curriculum of the University.

In Georgia and Kosovo, the Fund supported the facilitation of workshops and seminars in churches on family planning and reproductive health. In September 2009, a regional Consultation bringing together over 50 faith-based representatives, many of which had had partnered with national UNFPA offices, to successfully launch the Eastern Europe and Central Asia Interfaith Network for Population and Development.

ASIA and the Pacific

UNFPA supports the Fiji Council for Social Services and the Pacific Council of Churches to introduce sexuality education as a part of the Christian school's extracurricular activities. In addition, UNFPA provided funding for a series of seminars, carried out in coalition with the Fiji Council for Social Services, on preparing for marriage, with a focus on gender equality. UNFPA also contributed resources and technical assistance on women and HIV/AIDS initiatives through the Pacific Council of Churches.

In Bangladesh, UNFPA trained religious leaders, including 300,000 Muslims, 3,000 Hindus, and 280 Buddhists, to work as advocates on safe motherhood, gender based violence, and reproductive health issues. A UNFPA-sponsored conference was held in India in which religious leaders addressed the issue prenatal sex selection.

While in Thailand, UNFPA supported a pilot project in the Southern Muslim communities of Pattani Province, which promoted adolescent health and reproductive rights. Initiated by Planned Parenthood Association of Thailand and with the support of UNFPA, the project focused on out-of-school Muslim youth, by using peer educators. The project has enlisted the cooperation of religious leaders and by taking an Islamic perspective on issues of reproductive health and male responsibility, helped sensitize the influential Provincial Islamic Council on the importance of reproductive health education.

Many of UNFPA's Asia and Pacific-based partners convened in May of 2008 in a regional consultation in Kuala Lumpur, Malaysia. An important series of discussions were held, often heated and always passionate, between and among the various religions represented, and all focused around sharing the range of activities they were themselves carrying out on reproductive health, gender equality and migration and census issues. An elaborate list of recommendations, designed to provide some direction to both UNFPA offices as well as their faith-based partners, on enhancing the partnerships to better the range of services delivered jointly, was drawn up.[8]

Learning from the journey, and looking ahead to strengthened partnerships
Generally speaking, UNFPA-supported programs have been able to reach some of the most vulnerable and marginalized communities through partnerships with FBOs as well as other civil society partners. Some churches, mosques, schools, health units, income-generating projects, and youth organizations already have country-wide networks that are being built upon. Working with these networks lends a credibility and familiarity to new initiatives and reduces the perception of changes being imposed by external actors. This is especially important where initiatives seem threatening to community values.

Targeting specific areas of collaboration in areas where both partners have common objectives is another strategy that has proven to be effective on the ground. UNFPA has found that FBOs are open to discussing (if they are not already working on) reproductive health and rights, if issues are addressed with care and sensitivity.

One effective approach continues to be to provide evidence-based knowledge on issues, not only because this has proven to be an effective means of advocating on sensitive social taboos, but also because such knowledge is much in demand by the FBOs themselves. What are the latest figures? What are the latest medical facts and tools? What are the means of accessing these? And more such questions form the backdrop to what is required of United Nations agencies and international development partners. This is as relevant to data on infant and maternal mortality, as it is to the relatively more contentious realities of violence against women, and HIV/AIDS prevalence rates. This knowledge, and the tools and equipment needed, remain important resources with which to equip FBOs more generally, to tap into required ethical and moral positions. Indeed, many local leaders have changed their attitudes about UNFPA once they realized the value its approaches can have for their constituencies.

As per the principles of engagement noted earlier, UNFPA's global headquarters is keen to harvest the lessons learned and support national development processes in general, a feature that is applied to partnering with FBOs in particular. To that end, UNFPA convened and launched, in October of 2008, the Global Interfaith Network for Population and Development. What came to be known as the *Istanbul Consensus*[9] outlines the commitments that UNFPA and its faith-based partners made. In addition to a shared belief that "faiths share the same aims to safeguard the dignity and human rights of all people, women and men, young and old," there were specific vows to:

1. Work together to advance human well-being and realize the rights of all individuals with attention to women and young people;

2. Identify regional and national focal points, both in UNFPA offices and among FBOs;

3. Locate the interfaith network as a forum and means of exchanging experiences and learning from each other;

4. Continue to maintain strong regional and national networks supported by UNFPA country offices, feeding into a global network facilitated by headquarters, as a working modality to joint realization of the ICPD PoA.

FBO partners have also provided UNFPA with a list of recommendations, covering general advocacy, building of their—and our joint—technical capacities, as well as knowledge creation and management. A subsequent Policy Roundtable with internationally based FBOs, convened in August 2009, affirmed the Fund's Guidelines for Engagement and narrowed the range of areas to focus on until 2015, to maternal health and violence against women.

This focus is not meant to exclude other areas of partnership. In fact, an important UNFPA partner—UNAIDS—already has developed an elaborate *Strategic Framework for Engagement with FBOs on HIV/AIDS*, which was also completed and launched at the Parliament of World Religions in 2009. The UNAIDS Strategic Framework lays out in significant detail the areas and range of complex activities which AIDS irrevocably connects to (and there are very few domains indeed, where the disease, and those infected and affected by it, have no connections), and as such, provides an excellent framework for UNFPA's work in many of its own reproductive health areas.

While there are many lessons learned for UNFPA in its legacy of partnerships with FBOs, only a couple will be noted here, which are viewed to have a direct impact on the Fund's long-term strategic engagement.

Reaching out to FBOs is a learned skill, a strategic policy decision, and a conundrum

It was already noted earlier that the world of religion is complex and varied, as is the reality of FBOs. Try as we can to narrow down the domain to health service providers with a like-minded attitude (on and for human rights), to develop guidelines, to document the lessons and cases of success, and to develop indicators, the challenges remain in language, attitudes, perceptions of each other, and even in tempo of discussions and activities. But most of all, a major challenge resides in the global political dynamics which we are all part of.

Dealing with these different approaches requires significant skills on the part of all staff. Simple acknowledgment of the importance of partnering with NGOs and FBOs is not an automatic qualification in the skills required to identify, document, and, most critically, negotiate with these partners, especially when no two are alike.

Then, there is the conundrum: on the one hand, we must continue to advocate for partnerships, not only because these are critical service providers to the growing numbers of humanity's needy in times of dwindling resources, but because these are critical agents of change with moral, social and economic impact. On the other hand, the lines between religion, politics, and social advocacy are becoming increasingly blurred in contemporary realities where religion has become a force to be reckoned with—and its agents are not always saints.[10]

What can we say—and do—for instance, to those who will maintain that the same relief service providers may be engaged in supporting communities from within which grow, or who have connections with, radical elements?[11] What is the argument to be made when the same FBOs that are providing life-saving services may also be proselytizing their religious dogmas? Further, how can we continue to maintain drawing a line between health care service provision and political activism if that demarcation becomes increasingly difficult to draw on the ground? Indeed, which one of us has the resources to keep track of each and every non-governmental counterpart over time, and to trace changes in attitudes, range of activities, and shifts therein?

In fact, these are rhetorical questions. Because the answers are obvious: we can, we do, and we will endeavor to train our staff appropriately, but we must realize that on our own, we cannot do all that it will take to strengthen the partnerships. There are inevitable fault lines, which beg the question that at the very least, we have to coordinate our outreach internally and externally.

Partnerships with FBOs would be significantly enhanced through collaboration with UN sister agencies—i.e., a system-wide reservoir of deliberations, systematic monitoring and evaluation, and support—as well as by leveraging key trusted FBO partners as advisors and advocates

Without a doubt, "keeping track" and supporting each other, or trying to, will require deliberate communication efforts within the one United Nations agency—which, regardless of the size of the agency, is not always easy. Moreover, a means of communication and information exchange among and across all of those who are reaching out to the same set of FBOs as partners is critical. This lesson continues to be learned by UNFPA at the national, regional, and global levels.

There are a range of successful cases where cooperating with other UN agencies, around a shared task with FBOs, has proven helpful to all, including the FBOs themselves. Most recently, an initiative pioneered and supported by UNAIDS to convene a high-level summit of religious leaders on AIDS, together with two FBOs,[12] resulted in an unprecedented constructive dialogue and engagement not only with and between the religious leaders, but also with people living with HIV as well as intravenous drug users organizations. The Summit, which resulted in a progressive statement signed by all the leaders gathered—a feat which would have been impossible to obtain a few years earlier—was a testament to how UN agencies and FBOs can partner toward a shared objective constructively and with important and far-reaching results.[13]

UNFPA supported both UNAIDS as well as the FBOs in suggesting members of its interfaith networks, and advising on aspects of the design and overall approach. Inter-agency collaboration around FBO engagement has therefore become a mantra within UNFPA, and a rationale for investing significantly in ensuring a common platform and means for sharing of ideas, results of engagement, FBO networks, and more.

The *Inter-Agency Task Force on FBO Engagement* today is comprised of at least ten such partners,[14] with differing levels of membership and commitment. While this newly established mechanism has some ways to go to gain as much credibility and present a record of joint engagement on a par with other such inter-agency mechanisms, the mere fact that it exists today is a testament to the importance of the issue of partnerships with FBOs within the United Nations system. This is especially true for UNFPA, which, under the guidance and stewardship of its current leadership, has steered the organization to deliberate and strategic partnerships with FBOs, within the parameters of the human rights mandate of the United Nations as a whole.

UNFPA seeks to grow stronger and wiser over the years in its efforts to support national development processes with governments and civil society counterparts. Each day brings new learning with important policy and mandate consequences, but also with implications on how UNFPA carries out its development mandate. It is this impact on *developmental approaches* which UNFPA has sought to identify, study, and assess—and continues to do so. This is why UNFPA claims to have a unique developmental approach—one which integrates culture (and cultural agents of change) into strategic appreciation of gender dynamics, and effective realization of human rights.

Similarly, the collective thought and action behind the partnerships with the FBOs is bound to have an impact on the way development is made more generally and will be explored further in the concluding sections of this journal issue.

Notes

1. Azza Karam serves as the Senior Technical Advisor to the Fund, on Culture, and is based in the New York Headquarters. This article, although describing the work of UNFPA, contains the opinions of the author alone and does not necessarily reflect those of the Fund, its staff, Executive Board members, or any other Member State.
2. A human rights–based approach to programming is one that is built on a consensus achieved by all the United Nations system that requires consciously and systematically paying attention to human rights in all aspects of program development. It strives to secure the freedom, well-being, and dignity of the people within the framework of essential standards and principles, duties, and obligations, and with the provision of mechanisms to guarantee that entitlements are safeguarded and attained. As a backdrop to its broader mandate on peace and security, and on human development, human rights are a foundational and guiding doctrine for the organization's work and accountability.
3. See UNFPA's flagship State of World Population Report, of 2008, entitled Reaching Common Ground: Culture, Gender and Human Rights [UNFPA:2008].
4. For more details, see http://www.unfpa.org/culture/culture.htm.
5. Culture Matters to Development: it is the "How" and not the "Why" and "What" Traverse Lecture By Thoraya A. Obaid, 13 December 2005. http://www.unfpa.org.
6. For more details and case studies, please see the first of what eventually became a series and signature set of publications outlining the Fund's work linking culture and development: Culture Matters http://www.unfpa.org/public/publications/pid/1430.
7. From UNFPA's Guidelines for Engaging FBOs as Cultural Agents of Change (UNFPA, 2008), p. 1, http://www.unfpa.org/culture/docs/fbo_engagement.pdf.
8. See the Report of the Regional Consultation at: http://www.unfpa.org/public/publications/pid/2562.
9. See the full report of this Global Forum, including the Istanbul Consensus, at http://www.unfpa.org/public/op/edit/publications/pid/4501.
10. I have elaborated extensively on the relationship between religion and politics in other publications, e.g., *Transnational Political Islam: Religion, Ideology and Power* (London: Pluto, 2004).
11. By "radical" here it is meant, for instance, those who advocate against any means of family planning and decry any attempt to provide comprehensive reproductive health care services as "anti-religious" and/or may even urge that those who provide such services should not receive any governmental support. Other examples are those who advocate against the work of the United Nations as "a tool for foreign domination" and may even go so far as to blow up its buildings and kill its own staff in the process.
12. The two specific FBOs here are the Ecumenical Advocacy Alliance and the Dutch Catholic development organization—Cordaid. The initiative was strongly supported by the Dutch government, which has also been a strong backer of cultural outreach, following the examples of the Swiss government pioneers (as far as UNFPA is concerned), as well as the Swedish, Spanish, and German governments.

13. For more details on the Summit and its outcomes, see http://www.e-alliance.ch/en/s/hivaids/summit-of-high-level-religious-leaders/.

14. See the full list of UN and international multilateral partners of this Inter-Agency Task Force, and the reports of their consultations, at http://www.unfpa.org/public/pid/1352 and http://www.unfpa.org/public/publications/pid/4974.

CROSSCURRENTS

CHILD RIGHTS ORGANIZATIONS AND RELIGIOUS COMMUNITIES
Powerful Partnerships for Children[1]

Stephen Hanmer[2]

The instinct to care for children comes from deep within the teachings and spiritual vision of all religious traditions, which motivates people of faith to make the commitment to take practical actions for children. Fulfilling these commitments requires the collaborations of religious communities with each other, and with other partners, because these challenges cut across all religions and are too great for any one group to handle alone.[3]

Religious communities play a key role for the care and protection of children and have been a key partner to the work of many child rights organizations. Throughout the world, child rights organizations, including the United Nations Children's Fund (UNICEF), are working with religious communities of all faiths to address the well-being of children in areas ranging from health care and education to HIV and AIDS to protection from exploitation and abuse.

This article explains why it is important for child rights organizations to work with religious communities, provides examples of successful work with religious communities (in particular UNICEF's work with religious communities), discusses the main challenges of such partnerships and proposes what can be carried out to further effective engagement. In this article, religious communities refers to both men and women religious actors and structures within religious traditions and organizations at all levels—from local to global. These include grassroots and local communities, leaders, scholars, practitioners, youth groups, women of faith networks, faith-based organizations and denominational, ecumenical and intra-religious umbrella organizations, and networks.[4]

Why partner with religious communities?
As the United Nations Children's agency responsible for promoting the care, protection, and rights of children all over the world, UNICEF works in all types of contexts and in areas ranging from health to nutrition, water and sanitation, to education, HIV and AIDs, and protection of children from violence, exploitation, and abuse. Partnerships with key actors, such as civil society, and government, are a central feature of UNICEF's efforts to promote the rights of children. Indeed, it has long been recognized at UNICEF, as it has throughout the United Nations, that achieving the Millennium Development Goals depends on working in partnership with all sectors of society. Key among these essential partners is religious communities.

With their extraordinary moral authority and power, religious communities are able to influence thinking, foster dialogue, and set priorities for members of their communities. As those who are often the first to respond to problems, religious communities have the trust and confidence of individuals, families, and communities.[5]

From the smallest villages to the largest cities, and from districts and provinces to national and international levels, religious communities offer large networks for the care and protection of children and the safeguarding of their rights. The role of religious communities tends to be especially important at the family and community levels, which international organizations and governments are generally less able to reach effectively.[6] With almost five billion people belonging to religious communities, the potential for action is substantial.

Child rights organizations, including UNICEF, are guided by the Convention on the Rights of the Child, the most comprehensive legal instrument for the protection of the rights of the child. There is often a misperception that the language of the Convention on the Rights of the Child is contrary to religious beliefs. But the Convention on the Rights of the Child, which was adopted by the United Nations General Assembly in 1989 and ratified more quickly and widely than any other human rights instrument, was not created in a vacuum:

The Convention on the Rights of the Child reflects a vision of children in which children are social actors, members of a family and a community, with rights and responsibilities appropriate to their age and stage of development. This holistic vision of the child, as well as the principles of justice, humanity and dignity articulated in the articles of the Convention on the Rights of the Child, corresponds with the visions and principles of the world's religious traditions. As a universal statement of consensus about how children should be treated, the Convention on the Rights of the Child was informed by, and reflects, the deeply held values embedded in major religious traditions.[7]

Key components of the Convention on the Rights of the Child that connect with major religious traditions include:[8]
1. Fundamental belief in the dignity of the child;
2. High priority given to children and the idea of rights and duties of all members of society toward them;
3. A holistic notion of the child and a comprehensive understanding of his or her material emotional and spiritual needs; and,
4. The importance given to family as the best place for the upbringing of the child.

There is strong consensus across religious traditions about the inherent dignity of every child. At the 2006 Religions for Peace World Assembly in Kyoto, Japan, almost 1,000 religious leaders from all world Religions adopted the 'Multi-Religious Commitment to Confront Violence Against Children' (Kyoto Declaration) in which they stated that "We find strong consensus across our religious traditions about the inherent dignity of every person, including children . . . . Our faith traditions take a holistic view of a child's life, and thus seek to uphold all the rights of the child in the context of its family, community and the broader social, economic and political environment. All children hold these rights equally and we must ensure that boys and girls have equal opportunities to enjoy these rights, particularly education, protection, health, social development and participation. Our religious communities are blessed to be multi-generational, and we must use this to support the active participation of children in their own development and to address issues of violence."[9]

Success in engaging religious communities

Throughout the world, religious communities are in the vanguard of promoting actions to ensure children survive and thrive to adulthood. In clinics and schools, meeting places, youth groups, clubs, and of course temples, churches, mosques, and synagogues, they provide health care for poor families, schooling for vulnerable children, love, and support to children and young people affected by AIDS, and skills programs for young people. Their collective reach and impact is enormous. For example, the fiscal contribution of faith-based volunteers throughout Africa to address HIV and AIDS was estimated to be worth U.S.$5 billion per annum in 2006, an amount similar in magnitude to the total funding provided for HIV and AIDS by all bilateral and multilateral agencies.[10] Many of these interventions take place in close collaboration with civil society, governments, and United Nation agencies, such as UNICEF.[11]

UNICEF has a long history of working across the globe with religious communities of all faiths on far ranging issues that affect children. The following are a few examples in different areas of work reflecting the diversity of interventions and religious actors.[12] While the examples are taken mostly from UNICEF's experiences, the potential for these types of partnerships extend to other child rights organizations, many of which already extensively work with religious communities.

Child protection

In Egypt, Al-Azhar University and UNICEF jointly developed a manual, "Children in Islam, Their Care, Protection and Development," designed to underscore how the care, protection, and development of children is central to Islam. The manual includes research papers and extracts of Koranic verses, Hadiths and Sunnas, that provide useful guidance on children's rights to such things as health, education, and protection. Published in 2005 in Arabic, French and English, the manual has been widely distributed and used as a tool for theologians and imams, child rights and welfare workers, health care providers, educators, policy makers and others involved in promoting and protecting the rights of children. It has helped combat the erroneous belief that the Convention on the Rights of the Child goes against the basic tenets and beliefs of Islam.

For example, the manual has helped change the misperception that religion backs female genital mutilation/cutting, some form of which between 100 and 140 million girls and women worldwide have undergone. In Egypt, the Grand Sheikh of Cairo's Al-Azhar mosque, Sayyed Mohammad Tantawi, a prominent Muslim religious leader, and the Coptic Patriarch Pope Shenouda III, have both declared that female genital mutilation/cutting has "no foundation in the religious texts" of either Islam or Christianity. In June 2007, the Egyptian Grand Mufti Sheikh Ali Gomaa made a statement that the custom is prohibited in Islam.

In Mauritania, where corporal punishment is widespread and considered a suitable discipline method in both Koranic and secular schools, as well as families, UNICEF worked with the Imams' and Religious Leaders' Network for Child Rights, which carried out a study that concluded that corporal punishment has no place in the Koran, and thus has no place in Islam. The results of the study formed the basis of a *fatwā* (a religious opinion issued by an Islamic authority) barring physical and verbal violence against children in the educational system, as well as in the home.

Other UNICEF partnerships with religious communities included a Child-Friendly Local Church Communities initiative with the National Council of Churches in the Philippines, which included the publication of bible-based study guides on children's rights and integration of child rights into Sunday homilies, and a partnership with key religious leaders in Iran that developed a publication on "Discipline without Violence: Child abuse from the point of view of Shi'ism.

At the 2006 Religions for Peace World Assembly in Kyoto, Japan, almost one thousand religious leaders from all world religions adopted the 'Multi-religious Commitment to Confront Violence against Children' (Kyoto Declaration). The Kyoto Declaration outlines ways religious communities can work to eliminate violence in line with the recommendations from the United Nations Secretary-General Study on Violence against Children.[13]

Health

There are many global health initiatives, such as the push to eradicate polio, that have benefited significantly from social mobilization activities by religious communities. Several years ago in Nigeria, which is one of the last battlegrounds in the fight against polio, unfounded rumors in northern Nigeria about the safety of the oral polio vaccine stopped the immunization campaign, threatening to undermine the entire global eradication effort. UNICEF and other agencies worked closely with religious leaders for them to directly address their own communities to counter the rumors and get the campaign back on track.

In the Democratic Republic of the Congo, UNICEF is working with five of the largest Christian, Muslim, and Traditional religious groups to promote at household and community levels key child survival practices, such as exclusive breastfeeding, hand washing, immunization, and use of insecticide-treated mosquito nets. The five groups were strategically selected based on their credibility and capacity to promote behavior and social change, as well as their representation of a vast majority of the Congolese people. Together, their networks have the potential to reach more than half of the estimated 65 million people in the Democratic Republic of Congo.

During the Civil War in El Salvador, the Catholic Church negotiated a ceasefire to allow children on both sides of the conflict to be immunized. Similar efforts have been replicated in other conflict affected countries, such as Sri Lanka and Sudan. In Ethiopia, UNICEF partnered with the Ethiopian Orthodox Church so that at baptisms caretakers are asked by priests about the immunization status of the child and encouraged to complete the vaccination schedule within the child's first year.

Education
In Afghanistan, development and humanitarian agencies works closely with religious leaders to promote key programs including girls' education and child health. Imams regularly promote girls' enrolment, national immunization days, and other health campaigns through Friday worship across Afghanistan. In areas with limited school and medical facilities, mosques are used as classrooms and immunization centers.

HIV and AIDS
Through its Regional Buddhist Leadership Initiative Sangha Metta ("compassionate monks"), UNICEF has involved a growing number of Buddhist monks, nuns and lay teachers in the Mekong sub-region and as far away as Bhutan in the Buddhist response to HIV and AIDS prevention and care. What began as a small number of committed monks and nuns has

grown into an outstanding outreach program. Buddhist leaders are employing ideas and skills they have gained through the initiative to carry out low-cost, sustainable prevention and care activities in their local communities. They have been involved in prevention programs with young people, spiritual counselling, and supporting vulnerable families and children affected by HIV and AIDS.

The same collaborative structure was later used in the fight against avian influenza. In Cambodia, for example, nearly 6,000 Buddhist monks and nuns, along with many Muslim and Christian leaders, attended 70 orientations throughout the country sponsored by UNICEF and the Ministry of Cultures and Religions. The religious leaders then were able to disseminate information through their visits to communities and when people visited temples.

Challenges of working with religious communities and what can be performed to further effective engagement[14]

Just as it is important to understand the strengths of working with religious communities, it is also important to understand the challenges of such work. In some cases, religious communities can promote attitudes and actions that present risk to children's well-being. As acknowledged by the nearly 1,000 religious leaders from all over the world at the 2006 Religious for Peace World Assembly: "we must acknowledge that our religious communities have not fully upheld their obligations to protect our children from violence. Through omission, denial and silence, we have at times tolerated, perpetuated and ignored the reality of violence against children in homes, families, institutions and communities, and not actively confronted the suffering that this violence causes. Even as we have not fully lived up to our responsibilities in this regard, we believe that religious communities must be part of the solution to eradicating violence against children, and we commit ourselves to take leadership in our religious communities and the broader society."[15]

It is essential for child rights organizations to directly address harmful traditional practices within religious communities, many times the best strategy being working directly with religious leaders, who then themselves work within their communities to eliminate such practices. Success in this area often requires separating what is cultural from what is religious, as was performed in the effort to promote the elimination of female genital cutting/mutilation, and in preventing harmful practices from being upheld in the name of religions that, in fact, do not support them.

Even with the best of intentions, religious communities may lack the technical knowledge and capacity to effectively ensure the care and protection of children. It is important to work with religious communities to increase their access to good practice and evidence-based approaches to support children. Organizations such as UNICEF have extensive technical expertise and field experience to provide such support, but it is essential the support be provided in a way that is understood by religious communities and within the structures of communication already in place.

It is essential for children's rights organizations and religious communities to have the adequate knowledge, skills, and attitudes to effectively engage with each other in constructive ways—for example to understand each other's roles, working methods, way of speaking and structures to help identify effective entry points for co-operation.[16,17] The language of religion and child rights may at times seem oppositional. However, a deeper understanding and analysis of each other's language can reveal greater commonality, shared values, and goals than may be at first apparent. "The fundamental values shared by most of the world's religions have informed children's rights. There is more common ground between religious and humanitarian belief systems than is often assumed, and the work of "translating" child rights concepts into the more commonly understood tenets and beliefs of religious communities has shown to have a very positive effect in grassroots child protection advocacy work."[18] Unless a concerted effort is made for religious communities and child rights organizations to understand each other's language and values, they risk being unable to see the areas in which they are in agreement and may lead to erroneous conclusions about their ability to work together on behalf of children.

It is important that child rights organizations do not favor one religious group over another. They must work to forge inclusive and, where relevant, multi-religious partnerships based on how best to promote the rights of children. As secular and non-partisan organizations focused on the well-being of children, many child rights organizations can leverage their neutrality to mobilize support from all religious actors and use their mandates to encourage all actors to champion children's rights. For example, UNICEF's global reputation as an organization dedicated to children, and its expertise and mandate as a secular and non-partisan actor, furnish it with a breadth of relationships as well as the ability to play an effective convening role in bringing together key actors—ranging from governments to civil society actors to religious communities—around children's issues at global, regional, and country levels.

Conclusion
Ultimately, the wide-ranging nature of promoting the rights of children calls for a multifaceted approach. It is critical that people from all communities work together to ensure that the promotion of children's rights is at the center of concern. Religious communities bring diverse strengths and assets to the efforts to promote the well-being of children and by forging links with child rights organizations, they broaden and enrich the network of involvement and impact.[19] As recognized at the 2006 Religions for Peace World Assembly: "None of us can address this problem alone. It requires partnerships, solidarity, and building alliances. Even as our religions have much to offer, we also are open to learning more about the development and well-being of children from other sectors, so that we can each maximize our strengths. We are strongly committed to fostering effective mechanisms for inter-religious cooperation to more effectively combat violence against children."[20] Similarly, child rights organizations, such as UNICEF, need to also further engage with religious communities, especially in contexts where religion plays an essential role within communities.

UNICEF is not alone in being committed to working in partnership with religious communities to ensure the care and protection of the world's children. It is widely recognized within the United Nations and by civil society organizations and the private sector—and among religious communities themselves—that solid, varied, and long-standing partnerships are essential to achieving internationally agreed goals such as the Millennium Development Goals. Much has been accomplished through partnerships between religious communities and child rights organizations and much more can be done. There is still huge untapped potential. If we can recognize that potential and be open to finding common ground even when it appears that traditions and customs are at odds, we can achieve much for the world's most vulnerable and marginalized children. It is essential for child rights organizations and religious communities to work together harnessing each other's strengths into a joint vision to support children.

Notes

1. The findings, interpretations, and conclusions expressed in this paper are those of the author's and do not necessarily reflect the policies or views of UNICEF.
2. Stephen Hanmer, Civil Society and Parliamentary Specialist, manages UNICEF's work with religious communities and parliaments. Mr. Hanmer has worked for the past twelve years in programs for vulnerable and at-risk children in the United States, Pakistan, Lebanon, the Occupied Palestinian Territory, India, Brazil as well as throughout West and East Africa. Mr. Hanmer holds a Bachelor of Arts degree in History from Yale University and Juris Doctor in Law and Masters in Social Work degrees from Columbia University.
3. World Conference on Religion and Peace, *Care, Commitment and Collaboration: The Role of Religious Communities in Creating a World Fit for Children*. The outcome report of a multi-religious gathering on the occasion of the United Nations Special Session on Children, New York, 6–7 May 2002, p. 7.
4. UNICEF and Religions for Peace, *From Commitment to Action: What Religious Communities can do to Eliminate Violence Against Children*, 2010, p. II.
5. Hanmer, Stephen, and Aaron Greenberg and Ghazal Keshavarzian. *Religious Communities take the lead for* Children. Dharma World 2009, April-June Vol. 36.
6. Ibid.
7. UNICEF and Religions for Peace, *From Commitment to Action: What Religious Communities Can Do to Eliminate Violence against Children*, 2010, p. 17.
8. Volkmann, Dr. Christian Salazar, "Why and how UNICEF cooperates with religious leaders in Iran," UNICEF, Tehran, February 2008. pp. 1–2.
9. Religions for Peace, *Multi-Religious Commitment to Confront Violence against Children*, a declaration made at the Religions for Peace Eight World Assembly, Kyoto, Japan, August 2006. For more on the role of religious communities to eliminate violence against children, see the UNICEF and Religions for Peace publication *From Commitment to Action: What Religious Communities can do to Eliminate Violence against Children*, 2010.
10. Tearfund (2006). Faith untapped: Why churches can play a crucial role in tackling HIV and AIDS in Africa. Teddington, UK, Tearfund. Cited in Joint Learning Initiative on Children and HIV/AIDS, 2009, p. 28.
11. Hanmer, Stephen, and Aaron Greenberg and Ghazal Keshavarzian. *Religious Communities Take the Lead for Children*. Dharma World 2009, April–June Vol. 36.
12. Some of the examples are excerpted from Hanmer, Stephen, and Aaron Greenberg and Ghazal Keshavarzian. *Religious Communities Take the Lead for Children*. Dharma World 2009, April–June Vol. 36.
13. For more on the role of religious communities to eliminate violence against children, see the UNICEF and Religions for Peace publication *From Commitment to Action: What Religious Communities Can Do to Eliminate Violence against Children*, 2010.

14. Some of the ideas in this section are based on a March 2010 UNICEF and Religions for Peace consultation on the role of religious communities to protect children affected by conflict.
15. Religions for Peace, *Multi-Religious Commitment to Confront Violence against Children*, a declaration made at the Religions for Peace Eight World Assembly, Kyoto, Japan, August 2006.
16. UNICEF and Religions for Peace, *Conflict, Child Protection, and Religious Communities: Enhancing Protection through Partnerships – A Literature and Desk Review* (working paper) (February 2010).
17. In Botswana, for example, a wide variety of religious organizations worked with UNICEF to develop faith-specific sermon notes and religious materials on specific children's rights issues that resonated within their respective communities.
18. UNICEF and Religions for Peace, *Conflict, Child Protection, and Religious Communities: Enhancing Protection through Partnerships – A Literature and Desk Review* (working paper) (February 2010), p. 26.
19. UNICEF and Religions for Peace, *From Commitment to Action: What Religious Communities Can Do to Eliminate Violence against Children*, 2010.
20. Religions for Peace, *Multi-Religious Commitment to Confront Violence against Children*, a declaration made at the Religions for Peace Eight World Assembly, Kyoto, Japan, August 2006.

CROSSCURRENTS

CONCLUDING THOUGHTS ON RELIGION AND THE UNITED NATIONS
Redesigning the Culture of Development

Azza Karam[1]

Given the wealth of knowledge and experiential insights shared in this special issue by a distinguished group of authors, an attempt at summarizing can only fail to do justice. Hence, this concluding section will instead draw on the key points that this array of perspectives inspires. The first section will briefly highlight the areas of general agreement between the different authors and what this points to more broadly in terms of development dynamics. The next section will tackle some of the most tenacious challenges and questions with request to partnerships between the United Nations and the world of religion. The third and last section will highlight some broader implications from a human development perspective, which rather than be conclusive, underline the need for further analysis and reflection as the relationship evolves.

A mutual need

With faith-based actors providing on average, anywhere between 30 and 60 percent of many countries' basic survival needs (especially in the humanitarian, educational and health fields) around the world, and given a serious global financial and economic crisis, pragmatism demands that international development re-evaluate the role of religion across the board.

The United Nations remains the only multilateral service-oriented body with a comprehensive remit and a mandate signed on to by all the governments of the world. As such, it is an inescapable feature of modern day development, governance, and humanitarian service. And while it has obviously been able to exist—and grow—the last sixty plus years, with relatively little systematic notice to religion and religious bodies, the arguments presented in this journal edition show that times have significantly changed.

The United Nations is historically a secular institution representing governments, and as such, there are some legitimate concerns to reaching out to "religion." Some argue that religion is simply too divisive and too complex. Others recall alliances formed between certain religious bodies and governments during critical UN conferences on reproductive health care, and children's and women's rights, and shudder at the "anti-rights" language and discourse employed. Others point to the targeting of the United Nations and subsequent loss of lives in Baghdad, Algiers and elsewhere, and the ongoing threats to the institution articulated by terrorists claiming a religious agenda.

The three sections of this journal, tackling the relationship between "religion" and the United Nations (UN) through academic and ideological prisms, as well as via perspectives from religious non-governmental, or faith-based organizations (FBOs), and the varied UN bodies, while remarkably varied in tone, themes and results, nevertheless illustrate the same argument: whatever the concern, religion is here to stay. And today's political, economic, social, and legal landscapes are engaging with religion in its multivaried forms.

These multiple forms of partnership, each form a different bridge in which two-way traffic flows. Thus, in the same way that FBOs are adapting to the outreach to the UN, the UN, in turn, is adapting its own partnerships and language to "religions."

The mere fact that this "conversation" about the relationship between faith(s), or religion, and an avowedly secular entity is taking place, points to a feature of the "ripple effect" these emerging partnerships are having. As several contributors have pointed out, the last ten years or so have seen a boost in the amount of partnerships between the United Nations and religions, specifically FBOs, in different countries, as well as at the global level. Moreover, there is a relative "normalization" of this interaction, which is taking place within the religions institutions themselves—as the scholars lay out clearly—in spite of the tangible sense of disappointment with the speed of this by some, urge for caution by others, as well as some skepticism about these, by yet others.

The range of articles showcased here in fact prove that the tide began to change, within the United Nations itself, as well as in the NGO world, over thirty years ago, when the first arguments for why and how religion is a feature of human development can be traced. In fact, religion, as social service and thus social actor, predates the existence of every modern institution of governance and social service we know today, as does religion as an ethos for political engagement and both war and peace building. This is alluded to in the presentations of the scholars, and further underlined in the range of perspectives showcased by the various faith-based organizations. The United Nations is thus no stranger to partnerships with religious leaders, albeit in an ad hoc and—relative to its other forms of outreach with "secular" civil society—more piecemeal manner.

Ongoing challenges

Confluence of religion and politics
Ten to twenty years ago, the confluence of religion and mainstream political activism was deemed by many scholars and politicians alike to be at best, a "lack of awareness of secular realities." Today, religion and politics are the stuff of many a course in several universities, not to mention adorning the headlines of plenty of books and publications. Religion and politics, the sacred and the political, and several other variations of the same theme are definitely "in."[2] And for good reason. With the collapse of the Berlin Wall and the Soviet Union came a near eclipse of the grand political meta-narratives of communism and socialism. Left alone as supposedly the victor, Liberalism eventually found itself stranded on the murkier shores of globalization, and significantly undermined by the global financial crisis. The global landscape is further awash with problematic political regimes, serious global economic disparities, global warming and debilitating effects on the environment, armed civil conflicts, all with transnational acts of terrorism and the fear of terrorist access to nuclear weapons, as icing on the cake.

Ringing in the collective global ears are the mantras of charismatic religious personas and the ethos of religio-political parties working simultaneously, it would seem, on the mind (providing new mobilizing ideologies), and the body (serving many people's economic welfare in the form of education, health services and even pension plans in some countries). Whether it is the Christian Coalition of the United States playing a strong role in the election (and governance decisions) of former administrations, the Hindu BJP Party in India ruling for many years and now in opposition, or the ongoing influence of Iranian religious clerics and rhetoric in the political decision making, the fact is, religion and politics are today's most infamous bedfellows. And from the oldest of human memories to date, this "holy union" has rarely been a happy one (Karam, 2004).

Furthermore, when considering the relationship between religion and the UN, there are already many UN staff lives which have been lost to targeted killings undertaken by terrorist groups in the guise of religion.[3] To date, the United Nations is still considered an enemy by some terrorist groups. So the confluence of religion and politics is not a theoretical concern, but one which has already cost the UN human lives as well as other resources. The link to security, both in terms of the security of those the UN staff serves, as well as the staff themselves, and the implications on maintaining this in terms of physical costs and related logistics, is not minor.

It is a risk to believe that any "control" can be exerted once ground is ceded to an ideology based on the implementation of "God's rules" or any absolutist values. And herein lies one of the biggest conundrums for secular institutions considering the engagement with faith-based or faith-inspired ones. But it may be an even bigger risk to ignore the need for a new form of development practice that can address the multiple challenges confronted today: a world order in transition, a financial system in obvious disarray, and a climate, the protective layers of which are, literally, crumbling. The old ways of addressing the needs of human development are simply not good enough.

Development as business: Take 2—with religious overtones

The emergence of some FBO-run programs, specifically around the partnership interests—and resources—made available by the United Nations and the donor communities, potentially mirrors what took place in the relatively "secular" NGO movements over fifty years ago. While there are seminal and unprecedented strides achieved by global civil society institutions, the outreach to NGOs worldwide has nevertheless experienced some drawbacks.

To name a few of these challenges, one can mention the systematic outreach to the very same group of NGOs no matter the area of engagement, some of whom maintain a questionable track record of management and delivery. The subsequence is a creation of a global elite of development NGOs, some of whom have clearly found this a lucrative business, but may even have become distanced, in credibility and legitimacy, from the communities they purport to serve. In addition, consequences in terms of increased suspicion of development assistance by some governments and other civil society organizations alike are still hampering development processes. International development practitioners do need to be especially alert to the potential pitfalls of market-oriented non-governmental entities—but this time cloaked in the garb of religion, and/or using religious discourse.

The potentially myopic practice of identifying a handful of FBOs as partners to diverse UN bodies on each and every endeavor related to religion should be discouraged. The world of religion is too vast, and the world of FBOs (from international, to regional, to national to community and village levels) is too complex and rich, to be reduced to a few "comfortable" entry points. Overly engaging religious leaders, at the expense of those actually serving their communities on a whole range of issues, is also problematic. As the contributors to this issue have highlighted repeatedly, one spokesperson for a religious institution is not a harbinger of overall legitimacy within entire faith communities. Moreover, as recent developments bear witness, religious institutions themselves, and their leadership, are facing seminal changes to their authority and legitimacy. These developments should encourage international development practitioners in general, and the United Nations in particular, to be cautious as to exclusively engaging with religious leaders. At the same time, focusing only on service providers, without assessing the perspectives and insights or religious institutions and their leadership, can be compromising.

What is required is a balanced outreach to communities of faith, predicated upon common principles, and constantly "double-checked" by a proven track record in delivering on services, shared commitments and promises. The standards of "delivery" cannot be uniform to all the UN system except in one area: human rights, as meted out in the Universal Declaration of Human Rights (UDHR). Where religious leaders and FBOs have shown a shortcoming in, on and/or through the prisms of this universal mandate, there should be a clear "no-go" area for the United Nations.

Whereas the failure of a few NGOs and individuals to represent and deliver informs an ongoing sense of caution about engaging with them, it would be, at best, highly problematic, if a similar "failure to deliver" came to be seen as somehow linked to one particular faith or another. In the context of the interlinkage between religion and politics, this form of "negative" perception or association could have serious consequences. This is, therefore, a danger confronting international development, which is too easily used to dismiss or distance development bodies from religions, but which should, nevertheless, not be underestimated.

Harnessing investments or diverting them—and what about women's rights?

Linked to the above is a very real concern reiterated by several secular partners of the United Nations. Namely, now that the United Nations seems to be acknowledging the value of partnering with FBOs more and is partnering with them; does this mean less resources for secular NGOs? This concern is particularly—although by no means only—articulated in women's rights circles and mirrors a broader fear.

The traditional partners of the UN system, since the first women's conference in Mexico City in 1975, were the secular women's NGOs. Largely thanks to their efforts and the fruits of their partnership, bringing NGOs into UN fora, gradually became a norm. Many of these secular and feminist NGOs had a long and difficult history of struggle with mainstream religious spokespersons and institutions which still find it difficult to accept an "equal rights" discourse. So it is not surprising therefore that many of these women's rights' partners of the United Nations are now wondering whether this appreciation of religion may come at the expense of access to badly needed resources for them, and worse, whether it may even translate into the United Nations adopting some of the conservative positions of certain religious hierarchies. Herein, again, lies the importance of adherence to the precepts and actions of the Universal Declaration of Human Rights.

These concerns need to be tackled head-on and not left to fester. The United Nations itself, under the leadership of Secretary-General Ban Ki-Moon, continues to provide examples of why an acceptance of the importance of religious actors more broadly is not at the expense of any human rights—and certainly not women's rights. There are at least a few strong indicators that should allay any of the above concerns. There are more women heading UN bodies today than ever in the history of the Institution. These women, from different parts of the world and varied walks of life, come with a distinguished record of service for—and some with a complementing record of activism in—human rights. Moreover, in addition to the many strides in honoring women's rights that the United Nations can and should be credited for, on October 2009, the General Assembly adopted a resolution which strengthens institutional arrangements in support of gender equality and the empowerment of women. Effectively, this Resolution (number 63/311) endorses and paves the way for the creation of a new body, or entity, that would ensure coordinated focus on and oversight around women's empowerment.[4]

Human development or developing the numbers of faithful?

There is a lingering concern, articulated especially in the first part in the conceptual discussions in this journal issue, of the tension between providing real and necessary services, and the potential "strings attached" to specific religious dogma, or proselytization. This is a real thorn in the flesh for many secular development practitioners, and the reasons go back in history to the pros and cons of missionary work and its subsequent linkages to colonialism. But these concerns are also linked to different tensions around rights, almost as though there was a juxtaposition between [a religious organization's] right to free speech, versus the right to food/water/shelter or whatever service is being provided for by the same organization.

Far from attempting to resolve this complex nexus, we would venture to posit that the needs far outweigh the concerns. In other words, the numbers of those rendered vulnerable through lack of access to basic needs, whether as a result of natural or man-made inefficiencies, may far outweigh the number of those succumbing to conversion as a result of services provided through religious organizations. And in the absence of any reliable statistics on the number of "forced" converts after they were fed, clothed, and given shelter and refuge, it may behoove the development practitioners to focus on mobilizing and leveraging as many resources as possible to satisfy the documented number of vulnerable people around the world. Although this is not to dismiss the concerns about "religious exploitation of vulnerabilities" in any way, shape or form, it is rather to stress that these concerns should be addressed in a more studied fashion and not stand in the way of important partnerships needed to address growing basic needs.

Equal partners or instrumentalized ones?

To date, some religious leaders and FBOs have vocalized "the fear of being used" somewhat more openly than their UN partners. Some representatives of the faith-based world have questioned why the United Nations and larger international community have "suddenly woken up" to their importance. Some have even voiced their unease that this may be another "passing fad," which would seek to maximize on their strengths, and even attempt to "change our way of doing things"—almost as though a covert attempt were at hand to secularize the religious.

But some within the UN bodies too are equally concerned that the outreach to the religious world may be misperceived or abused. And here it is almost as though there is a fear of an attempt to "religionize the secular."

This mutual suspicion is more or less to be expected after so many years of sometimes tepid and often, ad hoc, acknowledgment of each other. It is noteworthy that those (few) UN agencies with the longest track record of successful results-based alliances with FBOs are less worried about issues of instrumentalization. Sustained partnerships, with sharing of lessons learned, and acknowledgment of mutual strengths and achievements, have created a sense of trust and respect on both sides. And this formula of trial and error based on actual engagement around service delivery in the field, with a transparency of purpose, together with respect for respective modus operandi and accountability to joint agreements, appears to be the only winning formula available thus far.

Which United Nations and which "religion"?

Last but by no means least is the issue of the vastness of the two worlds. As of June 30, 2004, the total number of staff of the United Nations was over 37,000,[5] and the number of UN agencies, bodies, offices and departments easily comes to sixty—each with their own staff, and many with headquarters and field offices.[6] In short, the United Nations is a huge entity with multiple facets, and a plethora of forms, on every conceivable aspect of human development. Many FBOs often either refer to this organism as though it were one homogenous entity, or complain about the confusion engendered by so many bodies all being part of "the UN." This is a very real concern because unless there is a deep knowledge of the system, which many in the United Nations themselves struggle to acquire, it can take a lifetime to understand with whom exactly, and how best, to reach out to, let alone partner with.

Yet even with all this complexity, the United Nations remains relatively quantifiable and has one Charter. But the same cannot be said of the world of faith, which makes the UN behemoth pale into insignificance. So it is not surprise, therefore, that when the United Nations needs to consider its potential outreach to the world of religions, it can be stumped. The number of religions in the world alone, let alone the range of official and unofficial spokespersons, statements, affiliated charitable groups—official and unofficial global, regional, national and community-based organizations, not to mention background holy books and bodies of interpretation, historical and contemporary, all this can be beyond the understanding of some of the world's best scholars on the subject.

This should not minimize from the track record of partnerships established between various elements of the "two worlds" however—a feat which, clearly, cannot be underestimated. But it does point to, yet another, ongoing challenge.

A view to futures—redesigning the culture of development

The United Nations' positive history of working with governments and civil society helps it create a safe space for varied forms of faith-based service providers, and religious spokespersons, to engage one another in the interests of development. Support for such forms of multireligious cooperation could simultaneously enable the United Nations to play an instrumental role in gauging the legitimacy and credibility of those religious voices and endeavors which are calling for social cohesion and multireligious coexistence.

The co-editors, in an earlier co-authored Op Ed in 2007, argued that:

> Senior UN management should endorse an initiative to carry out a comprehensive assessment of the possible role of religious organizations. This could be followed up by moves to compile the lessons learned by UN agencies, to reach out to existing partners within religious communities, as well as to government-sponsored religious bodies. In line with UN reform initiatives, it would also be good strategy to put together an interagency team that could work with experienced non-UN partners representing international faith-based organizations.[7]

It is important to note that since then, one of the co-authors, i.e. myself, moved from the United Nations Development Programme (UNDP) to the United Nations Population Fund (UNFPA), which is one of the UN agencies with the longest legacy of programmatic service-delivery engagement with faith-based organizations, through its country and regional offices. Precisely because of the strong endorsement of the leadership of this organization, the documentation of partnerships we had called for was indeed carried out and the first edition was completed in 2008. Moreover, an interagency team, composed of representation of several UN bodies, in addition to the World Bank, has since been convened. This mechanism has provided an opportunity for some of the staff in the UN system to exchange experiences of engaging FBOs, news, and information about important related events, contribute to relevant reports of the Secretary-General, reach out to joint faith-based partners, as well as share relevant documentation.

One of the many important lessons learned through this interaction between UN agencies and faith-based representatives, echoed in the varied articles, is that there can be no one way for the United Nations to see the world of religion, and thus no one model, or method, of engagement. In fact, the calls to attempt to "systematize the engagement" across the entire UN system, made by the co-editors some years ago, may well be unrealistic. Instead, we maintain the importance of working together, across agencies and bodies, and with the advice and participation of key FBO partners, to exchange knowledge, document the partnerships, assess the range and outcomes of such partnerships, as well as monitor, evaluate and build on successes. These are critical to an informed approach to mitigate against and deal with the real and potential challenges.

It is also important to realize that the most significant strengths of these forms of partnership lie in the ability to impact on the culture of development itself, i.e., the way development is undertaken, as well as the attitudes and behaviors of development practitioners—whether secular or faith-based or a mix of the two. And the largely rhetorical question here is whether such change can be monitored and evaluated as per the traditional development indicators. Where the partnerships are around delivering humanitarian needs, then the traditional quantitative indicators used by most service providers, would be feasible. But what of partnerships that are targeted toward attitudinal and behavioral change? Clearly, these call for more qualitative assessment strategies, which will have implications on how programs, are designed and implemented from the get-go. What we are therefore advocating for, and potentially foreseeing, is that the engagement between these two actors will fundamentally alter the human development paradigms themselves.

In reflecting on the secular UN culture of development itself, in which the tendency may often be to see the obstacles—and particularly to see religion as one such obstacle—we are informed through the varied presentations and arguments, that there is another way to see things. A way which involves "appreciation," "celebration," "acknowledgment," "recognition," and "affirmation." In other words, a positive way to "do development work" which faith traditions—which are familiar with and indeed use such terms—can contribute to.

Amartya Sen, winner of the 1998 Nobel Prize for Economics, is credited for being the architect of the term "human development." This was already a paradigmatic shift which moved development from being exclusively limited to hard core economics, and added domains which takes into account behavioral patterns, to identify "social capital," i.e., he not only indicated that culture matters, but he set out, through numerous publications, lectures, and interviews, to show how culture mattered. As such, Sen set the trend of linking identities, to values and to social capital, and these in turn, to holistic human development. While cautioning that the linkages were not always positive—as several authors in this issue have also performed—Sen nevertheless changed development praxis, partly, by identifying social capital, and allocating a critical and defining importance to it.

The logic here is that where and when positive elements of faith both form and inform values and praxis, faith becomes part of social capital. Interactions between religion and the United Nations are therefore impacting on the formation and efficiency of social capital. In turn, these relationships contribute to the evolution of the human development paradigm generally, and the culture of development especially. And whereas these relationships and their outcomes are not—and will not be—linear, they are, nevertheless umbilical. The evolution of a new development paradigm located in positive social capital, will, in the words of the Undersecretary-General of the United Nations and Executive Director of the UN Population Fund, Thoraya Ahmed Obaid, "further the sense of ownership in and by countries" of their own development processes. But they will also contribute to changing the manner in which development as a whole is conceptualized, practiced, and evaluated.

This journal issue has been an attempt to delve into an area that clearly requires more in-depth research. We hope that by sharing the diverse array of experiences and the varied perspectives—both for and against mingling religion and the United Nations—we have attempted to complement some of the important work emerging in this field and shed light on important questions and issues requiring further discussion and assessment.

Works cited

Karam, Azza, and Matt Weiner, 2006, "You gotta have faith in the UN: Religion and the United Nations," *International Herald Tribune* October 24, available at http://www.nytimes.com/2006/10/23/opinion/23iht-edweiner.3258982.html.

Karam, Azza (Editor), 2004, *Transnational Political Islam: Religion, Ideology and Power*, London: Pluto Press.

Rubenstein, Richard L. (Editor), 1987, *Spirit Matters: The Worldwide Impact of Religion on Contemporary Politics*, New York: Paragon House Publishers.

Notes

1. The opinions expressed in this article are those of the author alone, and are not necessarily reflective of, nor meant to represent those of any UN agency, member state, Board, staff, nor broader UN-related constituency.
2. See especially Rubenstein 1987; Gustavo Benavides and Martin W. Daly (eds.), *Religion and Political Power* (Albany, NY, 1989); Peter L. Berger (ed.), *The Desecularization of the World: Resurgent Religion and World Politics* (Michigan and Washington DC, 1999); Pippa Norris and Ronald Inglehart, *Sacred and Secular: Religion and Politics Worldwide* (Cambridge, 2004).
3. Especially evident in the bombings of UN buildings in Baghdad (2003), Algiers (2007), and Kabul (2009).
4. There are already several offices within the United Nations which are tasked with various aspects of the women's empowerment and gender equality agenda, and indeed, attempts to mainstream these concerns have been ongoing since 1975 with varying degrees of success throughout the UN system. This new entity was strongly advocated for by women's NGOs for over eight years and is seen by many as an affirmation by the United Nations to systemically seek to secure women's rights and gender equality.
5. This figure was counting staff in "the UN Secretariat and special status units . . . holding appointments of one year of more . . . Of that total, 14,823 paid from various sources of funding are assigned to the Secretariat and 22,375 are assigned to other entities of the United Nations. In "Composition of the Secretariat: Report of the Secretary-General," UN document A/59/299 of August 26, 2004, para. 11. Clearly, this figure is not taking into account staff on shorter-term contracts nor the Peacekeeping Forces. Hence, at best, this is a rather conservative estimate.
6. See https://unp.un.org/AboutUs.aspx
7. Karam and Weiner 2006

CROSSCURRENTS
CONTRIBUTORS

Wande Abimbola holds the title Awise Agbaye, which means Spokesperson and Ambassador of Yoruba Religion in the World. He taught at three of Nigeria's universities, University of Ibadan, University of Lagos, and University of Ile-Ife (now Obafemi Awolowo University, Ile-Ife) for thirty years. He also taught more than ten years at various American universities, including Harvard, Boston University, Colgate University, Indiana University, University of Louisville, and Amherst College. He was President of University of Ile-Ife. Abimbola also served as Majority Leader of Nigeria's Senate and later as Special Adviser to the President of Nigeria. At present, Abimbola is the President and Founder of Ifa Heritage Institute, Nigeria, a tertiary institution established by UNESCO and the Federal Government of Nigeria to teach and research the indigenous knowledge of West African peoples. Professor Wande Abimbola holds a Ph.D. degree in Literature. He has written many books and articles on the literature of Ifa, most recently, a book entitled *Ifa Will Mend Our Broken World*. He is a Babalawo, diviner, and priest of Ifa.

Carolyn J. R. Bailey, born to Salvation Army officers working in Zimbabwe, is a fourth-generation Salvationist. She received a B.A. Literature from Wheaton College, Wheaton, IL, in 1983 and an M.F.A. in Creative Writing—Non-Fiction—from Columbia University, New York, in 1990. From 1990 to 1992, Carolyn worked with her husband at The Salvation Army's Chikankata Hospital in Zambia, teaching English grammar and essay writing to nursing students.

Carolyn writes, edits, and rewrites materials for The Salvation Army. She has worked with its National Social Services Department; SAWSO—Salvation Army World Service Office; National Publications Office; and National Christian Education Department. Her projects range from anti-sexual trafficking programs to teaching parenting in drug and alcohol rehabilitation programs to building community capacity to care for orphans and vulnerable children. Carolyn is currently writing high school–level curriculum on doctrine, theology, and distinctive practices for The Salvation Army's National Christian Education department.

Josef Boehle is Research Fellow in Globalization, Religion and Politics at the Department of Theology and Religion and Coordinator of the UNESCO Chair in Interfaith Studies at the University of Birmingham. In recent years, he participated in the *Conference on Interfaith Cooperation for Peace* in June 2005 at the UN, the *High-level Dialogue on Interreligious and Intercultural Understanding and Cooperation for Peace* of the UN General Assembly in October 2007, as well as the first and second UN *Alliance of Civilizations Forum* (in 2008 and 2009).

Dr. Boehle's field of research is intercultural, interreligious dialogue and cooperation in a global age, focusing on international organizations and movements. He has worked with international interreligious organizations and has a wide experience of transnational civil society and issues of interreligious cooperation. Presently, he is writing a book on *Religion in a Global Age*.

Jean Duff is Executive Director of the Center for Interfaith Action on Global Poverty (CIFA), whose mission is to increase the collective impact of the religious sector on global poverty. From 2005 to 2008, as Deputy Director of the Center for Global Justice and Reconciliation, she led the Washington National Cathedral's global poverty program, focusing on Malaria and Gender Justice. She holds graduate degrees in clinical psychology and in epidemiology, as well as certificates of continuing education from Harvard and Wharton business schools.

Stephen Hanmer, UNICEF Civil Society and Parliamentary Specialist, manages UNICEF's work with religious communities and parliaments. Mr. Hanmer has worked for the past twelve years in programs for vulnerable and at-risk children in the United States, Pakistan, Lebanon, the Occupied Palestinian Territory, India, Brazil, as well as throughout West and East Africa. Mr. Hanmer holds a Bachelor of Arts degree in History from Yale University and Juris Doctor in Law and Masters in Social Work degrees from Columbia University.

James Heft is a priest in the Society of Mary, an educator, author, and leader for twenty years in Catholic higher education. After finishing his doctoral studies in historical theology at the University of Toronto, he spent many years at the University of Dayton. There, he served as Chair of the Theology Department, Provost of the University, and then Chancellor. He left the University of Dayton in the summer of 2006 to work on a dream he has had for two decades: the foundation of an Institute for Advanced Catholic Studies. Fr. Heft and his associates quickly concluded that The University of Southern California in Los Angeles was the perfect site for the Institute. He now serves there as the University's Alton Brooks Professor of Religion and President of the Institute for Advanced Catholic Studies.

Recent publications of the Institute include *Passing on the Faith: Transforming Traditions for the Next Generation of Jews, Christians and Muslims* (Fordham University Press, 2006); and *Beyond Violence: Religious Sources of Social Transformation in Judaism, Christianity and Islam* (Fordham University Press, 2004), both edited by Fr. Heft, who is currently editing *Learned Ignorance: the Limits of Knowing*, which contains papers that grew out of a week's meeting in Jerusalem in 2007 among Jewish, Catholic, and Muslim Scholars, and *Catholicism and Other World Religions*, which contains major papers and critical responses of a series of lectures held on USC's campus during the 2007-2008 academic year.

Andreas Hipple is Deputy Director for Africa Programs at the Center for Interfaith Action on Global Poverty (CIFA), with principal responsibility for providing technical assistance to the Nigerian Inter-Faith Action Association and other initiatives in Africa. Prior to joining CIFA, he consulted on international issues for a variety of public, private, and philanthropic clients. He earned his B.A. at Carleton College and an M.A. at the School of Advanced International Studies (SAIS), Johns Hopkins University, and is a Ph.D. candidate (ABD) at SAIS.

Jeff Israel is a Ph.D. candidate in Ethics at the University of Chicago Divinity School. He has taught courses on religion and political philosophy at Northwestern University and Rutgers University. He has also worked for the Council for a Parliament of the World's Religion (CPWR) and was the general editor of the CPWR's "State of the Interreligious Movement Report: 2007." He is the author of Loving the Nation: Toward a New Patriotism, with Martha C. Nussbaum, forthcoming from Yale University Press. He will be teaching Jewish history and political philosophy at The New School in New York City in 2011.

David Little retired in 2009 as Professor of the Practice in Religion, Ethnicity, and International Conflict at Harvard Divinity School and as an Associate at the Weatherhead Center for International Affairs at Harvard University. Until the summer of 1999, he was Senior Scholar in Religion, Ethics and Human Rights at the United States Institute of Peace in Washington, DC. From 1996 to 1998, he was member of the Advisory Committee to the State Department on Religious Freedom Abroad. Little is co-author with Scott W. Hibbard of the USIP publication, *Islamic Activism and U.S. Foreign Policy* (1997). Little is author of two of the volumes in the USIP series on religion, nationalism, and intolerance (RNI), *Ukraine: Legacy of Intolerance* (1991), and *Sri Lanka: The Invention of Enmity* (1994). The RNI conference report on Tibet, *Sino-Tibetan Coexistence: Creating Space for Tibetan Self-Direction,* written by Little and Hibbard, also appeared in 1994. He has edited two recently published volumes, *Religion and Nationalism in Iraq: A Comparative Perspective* (2007), with Donald K. Swearer, and *Peacemakers in Action: Profiles of Religion in Conflict Resolution* (2007).

Azza Karam serves as a Senior Advisor, on Culture, at the *United Nations Population Fund* (UNFPA), coordinating global activities on Culture and managing the Global Interfaith Network for Population and Development. Prior to that, she was the Senior Policy Advisor at the *United Nations Development Program* (UNDP) where she worked on the Arab Human Development Reports. She founded the first Global Women of Faith Network during her tenure at

Religions for Peace, while also advising on interfaith development work in Muslim nations, and served as the President of the Committee of Religious NGOs at the United Nations. In various countries in the Middle East, Europe, and Africa, she has managed developmental programs, taught at universities, and published widely in several languages on democratization, human rights, global multireligious collaboration, and political Islam.

Kusumita P. Pedersen is Professor of Religious Studies at St. Francis College, New York. Her research interests include global ethics, interreligious dialogue and cooperation, human rights, and the relevance of asceticism to ethics, especially environmental ethics. She is the editor of a special issue of *CrossCurrents* on "Asceticism Today" (Winter 2008) and Co-Editor of *Earth and Faith: A Book of Reflection for Action* as well as the author of articles on environmental ethics, interreligious concerns, and Asian religions. She has been involved in the global interfaith movement for more than twenty-five years and currently is Co-Chair of the Interfaith Center of New York and a Trustee of the Council for a Parliament of the World's Religions (CPWR). She has been a student of Sri Chinmoy, about whom she writes in this issue of *CrossCurrents,* since 1971.

Natabara Rollosson consults for the United Nations Development Programme (UNDP) on the nexus between religions, climate change, and human development. He has consulted for UNICEF, UNFPA, UNOPS, and the United Nations Executive Office of the Secretary-General. He is currently focusing on the development of green pilgrimage cities, strategic religious investment, and religious forestry standards. He has advised celebrities on humanitarian assistance in Haiti, and he serves as an international coordinator for the World Harmony Run, founded by Sri Chinmoy.

Abdulaziz Sachedina is Frances Myers Ball Professor of Religious Studies at the University of Virgina, Charlottesville. Dr. Sachedina, who has studied in India, Iraq, Iran, and Canada, obtained his Ph.D. from the University of Toronto. He has been conducting research and writing in the field of Islamic Law, Ethics, and Theology (Sunni and Shiite) for more than two decades. In the last ten years, he has concentrated on social and political ethics, including Interfaith and Intrafaith Relations, Islamic Biomedical Ethics, and Islam and Human Rights. Dr. Sachedina's publications include *The Prolegomena to the Qur'an* (Oxford University Press, 1998). *The Islamic Roots of Democratic Pluralism* (Oxford University Press, 2002); *Islamic Biomedical Ethics: Theory and Application* (Oxford University Press, February 2009); and *Islam and the Challenge of Human Rights* (Oxford University Press, September 2009), in addition to numerous articles in academic journals. He is an American/Canadian citizen born in Tanzania.

Varun Soni is the Dean of Religious Life at the University of Southern California. He is also a University Fellow at USC Annenberg's Center for Public Diplomacy and a member of the State Bar of California, the American Academy of Religion, and the Association for College and University Religious Affairs.

Donald K. Swearer is Senior Research Scholar, Swarthmore College, and Associate of the Asia Center, Harvard University. He specializes in Buddhism in Thailand and Southeast Asia with a particular interest in social ethics and lived religious practice. Recent publications include *Becoming the Buddha: The Ritual of Image Consecration in Thailand* (2004), *The Buddhist World of Southeast Asia*, 2nd rev. ed. (2009), and *Ecology and the Environment: Perspectives from the Humanities*, ed. (2008).

Thomas Uthup coordinates research and education activities for the Alliance of Civilizations at the United Nations. Current major projects in the education area of the UN AoC managed by Dr. Uthup include a clearinghouse on Education about Religions and Beliefs, a Research Network, and the expansion of exchanges. Dr. Uthup's academic focus has been on the complex relationships between culture and society, with special attention to religious factors—especially Islam—affecting political behavior. Current research interests for Dr. Uthup include South Asian and Middle Eastern politics, religion and politics, and global mobility in the education arena.

Matthew Weiner is Program Director at the Interfaith Center of New York where he has worked since its founding in 1997. He holds graduate degrees from Harvard Divinity School and Union Theological Seminary. He is currently writing a book about interfaith and civil society. His writing has appeared in *The International Herald Tribune*, *The Wall Street Journal*, *The Daily News*, *The Chronicle of Philanthropy*, and *The Jerusalem Post*.

www.ingramcontent.com/pod-product-compliance
Lightning Source LLC
Chambersburg PA
CBHW040259170426
43193CB00020B/2942